COLLIDING WITH ORION

Colliding with Orion
Writing from Life

Chris Wise

Colliding with Orion
Writing from Life
Chris Wise

© 2017 Chris Wise
Cover by Stephen Gros

ISBN-13: 978-0-9983373-3-3

Weasel Press
Manvel, TX
www.weaselpress.com

Table of Contents

Section III: Form

Part II: Short Story

I dedicate this book to bad luck. Thanks for the inspiration!

1 Corinthians 10:23 "I have the right to do anything," you say—but not everything is beneficial. "I have the right do anything,"—but not everything is constructive.

PUBLISHING CREDITS

The author offers grateful acknowledgement to the following journals, magazines, musical score and full-length collection in which the poems and short stories herein were first published, sometimes in slightly different versions.

America's Patriotic Soul: "In the Name of Liberty"
A Voice, A Sound, A Rhythm: "Even Ironwood Rusts"
Blue Collar Review: "Buckling Love Seat"
Blue Collar Review: "Squinting Over Bills"
Civilized Beasts: "Almost Tender"
Civilized Beasts: "Meeting Leviathan"
Cowboys and Indians Magazine: "Brave, Clean and Reverent"
Cowboys and Indians Magazine: "The Wheelie"
Cowboys and Indians On-line: "Whiskey in a Ghost Town"
Generation 3: "New God Paradise Fisher"
Nerve Cowboy: "The Flowers"
Texas Beat Poets Issue for Texas University: "There's a Cloud Now"
Thirsty Earth: "A Moment of Peace"
Thirsty Earth: "I Never Spoke to Atlas"
Thirsty Earth: "Lecture of Soul"
Thirsty Earth: "Shelter"
Thirsty Earth: "Tapestry of Heads"
Thirsty Earth: "The Halls of Leer (A Province in Hell I have Found)"
Thirsty Earth: "The Well at Auvers"
Time for Singing: "The Earthly Tent Destroyed"
The Pilgrim Within written for Mixed Ensemble; preformed in collaboration with Alex Wise; Premiered at Washburn University March 28, 2009 included "Gravity," "I walk, "
and "The Pilgrim Within"
The Road Not Taken: "Iophon Speaks"
The Road Not Taken: "While the World Decays in Bright Confetti"
War of Art: "White Trash"

ACKNOWLEDGMENTS

Thank you to The Fabulous Billie Duncan and Winston Derden who helped me to edit this volume and to shape its text features. Their frank advice was exactly what I needed. Also, I'd like to thank them for all the events they've hosted and the many readings we have done together over the years. Thank you Larry Thomas, the Buffalo, for sharing your knowledge (and bourbon) so freely and being my friend. Your hawk eye was invaluable. Thank you Dr. Jan Haswell for asking me to consider how writers host readers and for attending so many of my readings in the early days. Thank you Weasel for taking a chance on me by publishing this book! Thank you R.T. Castleberry for buying the first ever copy! Thank you Connie Berger for everything you have done for my career. Thanks to my good friends Stephen Gros and Lupe Mendez for continuing to invite me to participate in *The Word Around Town Poetry Tour* and your other events. Thank you Ryan Harris, Keith Krause, and my brother Robb Wise for collaborating on many music/poetry projects with me. Thanks to my brother Alex Wise for writing such an emotionally powerful composition for mixed ensemble around a few of my poems and risking that I wouldn't blow the live performance that he had so much riding on. Thank you Amalia Ortiz for being a great friend and inspiration. Our dial-a-poem telephone project remains one of the most unique I have participated in. Thank you Laurie Chandler and Teresa Papanicolaou for our Saturday publishing parties. Without you, I'd be too lazy to keep so many submissions in circulation. Thank you Johnathan Moody for the incredible angles you find to enter a poem and for your great advice. Your Randy Savage piece is solid gold! Thank you Anis Shivani for being a rebel and having a blistering standard. To all my friends in slam—Outspoken Bean, Savannah Blue, Marie Brown, Rain, and Amir Safi (to only name a few)— thank you for moving me with your work. Thank you Gerald Cedillo, Jasminne Mendez and Black Snow for your great performances. Thank you Brother Said for showing me how a modern sonnet can kill when recited as spoken word. Thank you Dave Summers for making me a brother and ducking live fire at a south Dallas school with me. You are an icon. Thank you Stefan Sencerz for hosting so many great events and roasting me when I left Corpus. That is one of my favorite memories from the early days. Thank you Keith Perez for asking for a copy of all my work that time. Your simple question made me reevaluate my choices... for a day! Thank you Kim Gentry for exploring Yeats with me. Get back to writing again! Thank you Gulf Coast Poets for inviting me in and for being my friends. Thank you Joseph Machado and Dustin Pickering for including me in your events. Thank you Fran Sanders for all your hard work with Houston Public Poetry and for the opportunities you have given so many of us. Thank you Rich Levy for your work with Imprint House and sharing the Imprint House with poets. Thanks to Robert Clark for hosting the First Friday open mic for over 40 years and for all you've done with Houston Poetry Fest (with Gary Rosin and everyone on the steering committee). Thank you Jim at NOTSUOH's for being such a friend to the arts. Thank you Robin Davidson for including me in the team of poets leading the development of two city initiatives—an online directory of Houston poets and an anthology of Houston's best-loved poems modeled on Robert Pinsky's national *Favorite Poem Project*, as well as the Houston Poets Webpage. These are wonderful assets to the city of Houston. Thank you Larry and Petrice Godfrey for giving me the chance to create and host my own television show *The Crawl*. KH-TV.com is awesome! Thank you Ricardo Alanis, Joe Francisco, Joe B, and Rich Mills for recording and filming so many of my readings. Thank you Dennis Flynn for editing my early work. You are missed. Thank you Joe Wheat for pulling me out of the grease... my whole life! Thank you Brian Baldwin for sharing so many years of writing (two novels worth) and being my friend through the thinnest times. I hope you are well.

INTRODUCTION

I shall never forget the night I met Chris Wise. It was in 2010 at a coffee/wine bar in Houston, Texas, which was hosting the "Poetry Showcase ThoughtCrime" program coordinated by Stephen Gros. Wise and I were two of five featured poets on the program that evening.

I had heard that Wise was a "performance poet." I must confess that I was not too impressed with "performance poetry" at the time. Although much of it was unquestionably powerful when delivered through a microphone, its power diminished significantly when I saw the same poetry printed on the page. It was simply lacking in the craft so indispensable to the art of serious poetry. Just a few words into Chris's presentation that evening, however, I quickly realized that I was hearing something special. His staccato diction was riveting, fashioned of consummate poetic craft remarkably free of modifiers, ripping the listeners' ears like mellifluous bullets. Furthermore, it was suffused with the stories of gritty life, hard-lived, exactly like the lives of so many of those in the audience. The audience's reaction to his performance was electrifying and visceral, culminating in uproarious applause and shouts of "more, more, more!" I shall never forget Wise's performance that evening.

Wise is an experienced and highly regarded educator in an inner-city Houston secondary school. In this creative writing textbook, he infuses every page with the craft and actual-life-grit which characterized his performance that evening in Houston. Through the detailed explications of his own poems and stories based upon events from his own life, he immerses his reader deep into the intricate "mechanisms" of poems and stories, explaining the complex elements and terms of artistic craft so clearly in his examples that they hardly seem "complex" at all.

Although the majority of the poems he showcases are written in free verse, he also includes poems written in form such as the sonnet and the villanelle. The grittiness and true-to-common-life character of the book belies the consummate artistry of many of Wise's poems and stories, some of which first saw the light of print in distinguished and highly selective publications such as *The Road Not Taken* and *Cowboys & Indians: The Premier Magazine of the West.*

This accessible book is ideal as a textbook for secondary creative writing students, both those who desire to improve the power of their work written solely for personal expression and those who plan to further their study and practice of creative writing. Wise concludes the book with a comprehensive glossary of literary terms, clearly presented, and an extensive bibliography.

Larry D. Thomas
Member, Texas Institute of Letters
2008 Texas Poet Laureate

FOREWORD

It is rare to find in a skilled poet the art of a master teacher. It is rare to find in a master teacher a poet's love and feel for language. Even more rare is the instructive pleasure of listening to a poet who values readers, who is also a teacher who values students and speaks to them as fellow writers.

In *Colliding with Orion: Writing from Life*, author, poet, and teacher Chris Wise exemplifies these rarities. He maps out a complex dialogue with aspiring writers, not in the role of published expert but of a mentor who values their skill, passion, and potential. The subtitle—*Writing from Life*—captures the primary motif in that dialogue. With each model of poetry or fiction, Wise provides extensive levels of analysis in sections he calls "The Writer" (which trace the raw materials of experience that are the basis of the poem or story), "The Craft" (which analyze the mechanisms of expression and revision), and "The Invitation" (which challenge readers in specific ways to make art out of their own life experiences).

To facilitate this dialogue, Wise does not use the poetry or fiction of masters—material that is often the grist of creative writing guides. The only way that his insights can be honest and accurate is to speak from his own experiences of living, of imagining, of writing and revising. This is a courageous decision, since Wise must expose his own past experiences and "span of years and range of skills." He doesn't offer his writing as an example to be mimicked, no more than he recommends his life journey as one to be imitated. Rather, his purpose is to "hold a door open" to fellow writers on their own journey.

Whether explaining a single poem or considering two or three poems together, Wise first explains how the poem is rooted in the experiences of his life under the caption "The Writer." Some tough times, to be sure, pocked with poverty, violence, "trouble," as he says. There are also fond memories of his father and grandparents. Dozens of stories emerge, all comprising foundations and influences, but not yet art. Gradually there emerges one of Wise's tenets: experience (a.k.a. facts) do not by themselves speak truth. They must be transformed into language, and as Lawrence Langer reminds us, all telling modifies what is being told.

One of the most instructive aspects of this book is Wise's examination under "The Craft." Here he discusses both the writing process and the tools of the artist. Those tools are numerous and comprehensively explored: diction, pace, stanza structure, images, metaphors, similes, symbols, allegory, alliteration, word choice, character foils and dialogue, motif, juxtaposition, inference, dramatic irony, plus a myriad of genres. With each example, readers are not simply coached in the abstract. Rather, they are shown a specific example that is dissected and critiqued, and then challenged to try that mechanism in their own writing in the sections called "The Invitation." Here Wise provides the kind of mentorship that goes beyond simple encouragement. In addition to challenging readers to employ a device or revise with an ear to the music of a line, he poses questions for reflection. Wounds and scars are valuable, but is poetry the same as therapy? Is political poetry sufficient to make a political life? What is the relationship between poetry and music? What happens to a poem that is performed in public—how does the performance demand a change in form, in the structure of a line, in an effective motif that is heard and not read?

To engage in this dialogue will certainly be challenging, perhaps even hazardous. So why trust him? For one, Wise is an accomplished writer. His mature verses are often stunning (take for instance, "The Well at Auvers"). It isn't simply that he is widely published. He has worked at his craft, through thick and thin. He is at home in the devices, genres, and language of the artist. He is comfortable with even the strictest of forms (like the villanelle) and the seemingly foreign forms (as found in Chinese poetry). "Forms are freedom," he reminds his readers. Yet for all that, he is also an iconoclast. He serves no ideological or pedagogical master, yet he readily acknowledges the influences in his life—past masters, current poets, candid friends.

Perhaps most telling are the kinds of reflections Wise offers in the sections entitled "Consider this." Here his mantras emerge. First, always respect readers, he admonishes. Don't bully them with heavy-handed preaching. They will find their own spaces, generate their own judgments and feelings. Second, don't make yourself (or your characters) simplistically admirable. Readers don't need to admire someone so much as identify with them, find someone who helps them grow in self- knowledge. And third, art comes with revision. A step away from the raw materials of experience or feelings is a step closer to truth.

Colliding with Orion proves ingenious in its structure, tone, and content. It is not an easy guide to follow or a comfortable dialogue to have. The questions Wise poses are difficult (What *does* morality feel like? How does one shoulder the burden of remorse?) and the techniques he recommends are increasingly exacting. The bottom line, to his credit, is the belief that "every reader lives a life worth writing." And writing elevates those lives.

Janis Haswell
Professor Emerita of English
Texas A&M University-Corpus Christi

HOW TO USE THIS BOOK

I hope other writers are able to use my writing to recall their own moments and situations to write about and enter their own work.

The book is divided in two parts: **Poetry** and **Short Story**, with the poetry segment divided between sections entitled **Outlooks** (emotions and beliefs) and **Mechanism** (literately device and technique). I chose to use the word "mechanism" over the commonly used "device" because to me the word mechanism implies moving parts—like the inside of a mechanical watch. Mechanisms are working, dynamic, and complex, while the word device feels static and singular.

These sections are in no way comprehensive but are ordered in what I felt seemed most logical for a gradual release model, building towards short story writing.

The body of this book is composed of original poetry and short story examples with three sections of accompanying writing: THE WRITER, THE CRAFT and THE INVITATION. Most of the works stand alone, but some groups have a comparative or contrasting relationship, and these share THE INVITATION, but have their own THE WRITER and THE CRAFT segments at the end of the grouping. These icons indicate such groups:

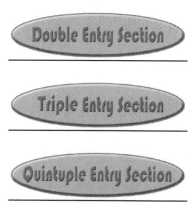

Double Entry Section

Triple Entry Section

Quintuple Entry Section

THE WRITER is my autobiographical connection that usually is inspired by or related to the work. A reader may notice that sometimes I show little overt imagination and just write down what happened. Other times, I begin with a kernel of truth and spin a very different fiction. At still other times, I cobble parts of one story with parts of another to create a more interesting work. After all, as a friend of mine used to say, "Just because it happened doesn't mean it was interesting."

THE CRAFT is a comment about a few techniques used in my work. The intention here is to invite readers to reflect over their own writing and consciously practice some of the ideas in their pieces.

Since I perform poetry as well as write for publication, I have included notes when appropriate about poetry performance.

Consider this:

The motive for writing always changes, but the concepts of what makes writing good do not. Good writing is effective no matter if it's poetry or prose. Only the considerations of the forms differ. For example, all music is music, but how we play a piano or a guitar differs in that they are different instruments. Each maintains the latitude of having peculiarities and opportunity for virtuosity all its own.

It is the professional duty of writers to understand what makes good writing effective so that they themselves can be more effective. These notes cover what I think makes good writing, particularly as they pertain to the included work.

Perhaps a note on register might be helpful when talking about craft. Register is the way we shift our language to conform to certain social contexts. If the register shifts in my writing examples and sounds a little more academic, stick with it, and don't let it put you off. I've added footnotes and sidebars so you don't have to go far for the definition of an academic word. More important than knowing any technical word is that you know how the mechanism works that it refers to.

Along with my own pieces, I offer connections and examples from mentor poets and authors who have influenced my work. I include these in the spirit of the intertextuality of literature, which builds from one writer to another through an echo of lines and allusions implying a great conversation and existing from the first works to now.

For example, consider Jerome Robbins (who conceived), Arthur Laurents (who wrote the book) and Ernest Lehman (who wrote the screenplay) all wrote *West Side Story*, a modern retelling of William Shakespeare's play *Romeo and Juliet*.

Shakespeare's Montagues and Capulets in *Romeo and Juliet* are also found in Dante's *Purgatorio*, Canto VI line 106.[1]

Dante, most likely, read Catullus[2] who created Lesbia (a woman the poet loves so deeply that he himself is defined by her), as Dante did Beatrice[3], as Shakespeare did the Dark Lady and the Young Man.[4]

As writers, we too are a part of this conversation. It transcends language, culture, country and time.

THE INVITATION directs writers to recall moments and situations that they might use to enter an original poem or a short story. This part says, "Yes you do have something to write about!"

I offer examples and anecdotes to spur my readers' natural egocentrism, so that when they relate back to self, they can remember a similar time and address the blank page with their own writing.

Everything readers of this book do (the voice, technique, etc.) may be totally different from what I present. I only hope to entertain these readers and hold a door open while they access their own creativity.

Every reader lives a life worth writing. **THE INVITATION** sums up **THE WRITER** and **THE CRAFT** by saying, "Here's how I did it. Now, you try."

---

[1] J.J. Dwyer wrote a compelling essay on the subject, titled 'Did Shakespeare Read Dante?' See Bibliography.
[2] Catullus (c. 84-54 BC)—Latin poet of the late Roman Republic.
[3] Beatrice Folco Portinari (1266-1290)—Principal inspiration for Dante's *Vita Nuova* also appears as one of his escorts in *The Divine Comedy*. It is said he only met her twice in his life but fell deeply in love her. After her early death at 24, he set about immortalizing her in poetry.
[4] Shakespeare's sonnets 1-126 primarily address a young man. Sonnets 126-154 primarily address a dark-haired lady.

Consider this:

When it comes to revising your work, understand that your writing is not your child. It's not even a waste product, a shed hair, something exfoliated. It is a creation of art to hold up and study in the light like a precious stone that has been cut. The difference is that its flaws can be refined along with the color and clarity of the work. But there's a balance.

You can revise the life right out of a piece, taking it from zero to one hundred and back to zero. You're finished revising when the writing stops being better and starts just being different.

The Work

The pieces herein are from a span of years and no doubt demonstrate a range of skill. They are not a collection of my greatest hits. Instead, I chose them for the functions they demonstrate with the hopes that they will trigger your writing. In the spirit of shared risk, I offer them from one writer to another—me to you.

We have worked hard to make certain that there are no typos in this book, but most books—no matter how diligent the writers and editors—have typos. So, rejoice if you find one. I offer them as something lucky—like a for leaf clover. (Hey, there's one there!)

POETRY

Outlooks

WINDOW PAIN

The window is where my headboard would be
if I had one.
The room is small and narrow, barely
big enough for a bed.

It's cold out,
has rained for two days solid,
and the window leaks.

My feather pillow is soaked, but
I am tired, and it is still better
than my head on a few dirty clothes
or my hands.
I've done that many times; it always hurts my neck.

Once the pillow warms to the heat of my
head, it won't be so bad.

The wind is loud,
but above the whistle of the crack
I can hear birds singing.

The Writer

Those years were life in the raw. But, that old trailer was good living, especially since I had a friend to split the rent with. The first place we split was a quadplex. It was so rundown they condemned it not long after we moved out.

We had our hard luck, but there was no need to complain. Everyone around lived in the same situation or worse. If anyone did pipe up, he or she was usually ridiculed to silence. No one likes a whiner.

The Craft

This piece presents a character living in a less-than-desirable situation but ends with a symbol of hope—birds singing.

The irregular stanzas have radical enjambment, rough edges and odd breaks to mimic the irregular, rough living conditions of the speaker.

> Enjambment is the continuation of a sentence or clause beyond the line break to create audible interest.

I included this piece to make the point that it is not up to the writer to tell the reader how to feel—ever. It's not up to a performance poet to overact a reading to cue the audience that they should feel a certain way (usually sympathetic or angry). That makes for a hackneyed performance.

It is for the writer to create a situation and leave it. Readers will find the space to empathize or not. That's their privilege alone.

The Invitation

Hard times are a fact of life. Figure out a way to discuss them without sounding as if you're so precious you don't deserve to suffer because we, who have taken life full on the chin and stayed standing, will never respect you. Besides, keeping a loser's attitude is a pathetic way to live.

With that in mind, write about a time you faced adversity.

Consider this:

When we read, we expect to identify with the main character. Give us someone we can get behind.

Readers are smart. If you paint a stark situation and demonstrate a character navigating the miseries of it, the reader will more likely feel empathy as they will recall their own sufferings, and with this memory, they will recall the strength that saw them through.

Those readers have bettered themselves because they slugged through life taking gut shots and head shots. Their suffering was more real than yours is because it was theirs. And they are all that matters. When writers host readers, they must remember this. Poor writing lectures an audience as if they have no idea what the writer has gone through.

WHITE TRASH

They called me White Trash.
Any other day I would have laughed,
but today I didn't.
They're Hispanic and own a boat,
have three cars
and a two-story house
on the canal.
Now I understand why their daughter
was told to "get rid of" me
when I came to visit.
That's what you do with trash.
They laugh at people
who live in trailers.
My best friend lives in a trailer;
we were roommates once.
I don't have the best manners.
I don't even have good clothes,
and I can't always afford two meals a day.
But I've served in the U.S. Army,
worked my way through college,
and I believe in being thankful
for what you've got . . .
even if other folks laugh
at the best you can do.
So if I'm White Trash,
I guess I come by it honest.

The Writer

When I attended Texas A&M Corpus Christi, I could use the college gym for free. I had a female friend I worked out with to help her lose weight. Working out with me, she lost fifty-five pounds. I was poor back then and didn't realize a person needed a designer line to sweat in. I will never forget the embarrassment of showing up in a stained, threadbare t-shirt and some gray sweat pants that I had left over from my days in the Army. They were all I had, so that's what I wore. Everyone else, of course, looked great, dressed to impress and barely sweating.

When I met my friend's parents, appearing as I did, they called me white trash and had her ask me to leave, not knowing—maybe not caring—I was the one helping their daughter feel better about living. That year, she went from feeling very depressed to modeling in a retro-fashion show.

Racism and judgments most often say more about the person they come from than they do about their targets. As writers, we can approach these topics with anger or enlightenment. I can't help what I am, and if that upsets people, the problem isn't mine—not when I usually do my best with manners and social etiquette.

In my early years, in Tulsa, Oklahoma, I often lived with my grandparents in a 740-square-foot home that dead-ended into a junkyard and train tracks. When they passed away, the house sold for only twelve thousand dollars. But we weren't trash. Grandmother kept a clean house and we kept the yard cut. My grandfather retired from the Tulsa County Sheriff's Department and the U.S. Post Office. My father sprayed crops, hung sheet rock, sold cars—always worked hard and taught me about hard work. They loved me and treated me well. Though we weren't well off, we were anything but trash.

The Craft

The basic structure of the poem is a contrast between the speaker and his antagonists. The first line sets up the problem. The lines that follow detail the antagonists' higher socioeconomic status and their judgments of poorer people like the subject.

As stereotypes are usually only textural in nature, I use dramatic irony to reveal for the reader what the antagonists did not know about the person they judged. I kept the diction simple to demonstrate a common character who readers can easily identify with.

We have all been too hastily judged, mistreated and humiliated at some point. My message in this poem is not that bad people pass judgement; I think we have all played their role at some point, if we're honest. My message is that they were myopic and wrong, and the shame was on them, not on the character in the poem.

The Invitation

Write about a time you felt misjudged, stereotyped, treated with bias or considered less than. Use the structure I used, or come up with your own, but try to avoid sounding like a victim. Readers don't want to identify with a whiner. Plus, complaints are easy and generally unimaginative. Instead, portray your situation honestly and the resolution (that's the reader's take-away) with grace.

There's A Cloud Now

He sat
afternoon to sundown,
cross-legged on a five-gallon bucket.
His sign:
    "Hopeless drunk
    Need food and beer."
He had a dog for a time—
a thin, rough collie,
and a friendship with a bag maiden
who frequented him for talk.
People were always stopping by to talk.

I haven't seen him for a while now.
I'm not sure if the cops finally ran him off
or if one of the terrible things
that often happen to street people
                                    got him.
His spot is empty.

I never had anything to spare,
except the nods we shared when I passed,
but they were genuine.
I recognized him
as a man
neither vermin, nor waste,
who—for his own reasons—
had declared himself *hopeless*.

I'm not sure what he thought of me,
but maybe he saw the same dullness in my eye,
and that's why
he nodded back.

The Writer

Several homeless people often gathered at the H-E-B Grocery Store near my apartment. They congregated at curb or gave one another rides through the parking lot in stray shopping carts. One man had the sign "Hopeless drunk, need food and beer." He kept a dog, as the poem says, and people frequently stopped by to visit him. One day, my friend came over and said he'd given the man a beer and doughnut. I asked him how the guy reacted. He said, "Well, he drank the beer and gave the doughnut to his dog."

In those days, life was catch-as-catch-can. I'd skip meals to pay bills. Money problems, tickets and fines, warrants for not being able to pay said tickets and fines—all common problems. I never looked down on the homeless around me. We weren't that far removed.

The Craft

This is a narrative piece with the stanzas grouped in a way that I had thought would pace the read. This grouping seems to want to change with every new reading I give it. The way it sits is simply where I've let it settle. I use dashes and broken lines for emphasis.

A stanza, meaning "room" in Italian, is a grouped set of lines in a poem usually set off from other stanzas with a line space or an indentation.

The Invitation

It's easy to live life looking down our noses at those with less. And it's a mistake, even insulting, to over romanticize them as modern, noble savages. Instead, try seeing yourself in what you judge.

Recall a time you felt judgmental. Write a piece in which you paint a situation that your narrator passes through, and as easy as it would be for him/her to negatively judge, you instead reveal an ironic, empathetic parallel between the speaker and the subject.

The Most Beautiful Woman I Ever Met

I picked her up at 6:30.
We went to see Phyllis Diller[5]
and the symphony.
I wore a tie and my nicest shoes.
She wore a very low-cut, expensive lace dress
that hugged her perfect body.
Blond hair was pulled up in an exotic wrap,
and her warm smile, as always, could make a poor man only dream.

We held hands.
I had never been to a comedy show or seen a symphony,
but knew
to spend time with a woman like her,
it was the treatment she expected.

I had worked many late hours,
saved all I could, skipping meals
and only sleeping in extra time I didn't have so I could afford tickets.
Of course, she didn't know that.

After the show we went to a park by the ocean.
Laughed at jokes we remembered
talked about what we were looking for in a relationship
and watched fishermen reel in small fish
like they were big fish.

We laughed a lot, got close at times,
but I wanted to be a gentleman for once.
I took her home,
walked her to the door,
opened the screen for her.
For a brief moment, it seemed she might have waited for a goodnight
kiss, bemused,
while I stood in the tongue-tied tension,
frozen, awkward, with the heavy screen glued to my hand,

---

[5] Phyllis Diller (July 17, 1917-August 20, 2012) –An American stand-up comedian.

until the moment passed.

I walked away kicking myself,
hoping there would be another time,
a second chance,
then drove back to my hot apartment
in a filthy part of town
where she would never go.

The Writer

I once met a goddess masquerading as a shot girl. I was a bartender, and I'll never forget stealing glances at her, too mortified by her beauty to approach. Then one day some drunken cowboy staggered over and asked her for a kiss. She gave him one. My goodness, my goddess was easy!

I learned that night to stop holding back. Had I "cowboyed up" and struck while the iron was hot, I might have failed, true enough, but at least I wouldn't have any regrets.

The Craft

The speaker in this piece makes quite a lot of assumptions about what the female character could want or expect because of his situation. These assumptions cow him, and his own timidity sabotages what could have been a romantic ending to the date he had sacrificed so much for. Instead, he is clumsy and self-defeating.

The first two stanzas illustrate the situation.

The third stanza reveals for the reader (through dramatic irony) what the lady could not have known and establishes the gulf between social classes.

The following stanzas detail the speaker's regret, with the poem resolving with a stark comment affirming the impossibility of the relationship.

The Invitation

Write about a time you felt out of place. Maybe your etiquette wasn't up to par, or the social circle knew you didn't belong, or your clothes were shabby.

Did you make some assumptions about members of the group that made you feel intimidated and less than them?

Was it social class and personal insecurity like my example?

Were the others in the situation all experts, but you were a novice?

Were you the only woman in a group of men?

Was everyone else of a different race, and you felt that you stuck out in an awkward or negative way?

> A foil is a character who contrasts with the protagonist.

Was it all in your head?

If you had acted differently, might the situation have ended with a more positive outcome?

Once you recall the instance, try setting up that situation. Let the piece evolve so that the reader knows what other characters in the piece do not. Give no indication with the foil characters that they would agree with the speaker's insecurities. This will help build tension in your work. Then, let the piece resolve with an insightful comment from the speaker.

Maintain that the speaker is an outsider throughout the work.

You may write an entire collection explaining how insecurity holds us back, and that it's risk-taking, not timidity, which propels us forward.

APARTMENT 3247

I hear couples come and go
in the row of apartments
down the hall.

I hear the rattling plastic
of their grocery sacks
and the murmuring of friends who come to dinner.

No telling what fine meals and imported wines they share.

I am poor with little to offer, so I hide alone in here.
Sometimes, I hear their music and singing,
and my floor vibrates with the levity.

I play my music, too
and sing songs I've written.
I strum them on guitar... but no one hears

or sings along.

The Writer

Some of us feel as if we're the loneliest people with the most friends. Secluded in a city of millions. Not around people, but besieged by them, swallowed and lost in the white noise of humanity with few deep connections, even though—in the bitterest of ironies—we crave these relationships most.

A motif is a recurrent subject, theme, idea or pattern in literature.

This writing may not be material we feel comfortable sharing, but it's real. Loneliness is as valid as happiness. So, not only is it okay to write about it, honest writers *must* write about it. To exclude this from our work denies a part of our own existence.

The Craft

This is an outside-looking-in piece. A basic contrast between how the speaker perceives the neighbors and how the speaker feels.

I use sound imagery such as plastic sacks, conversations, music and singing to emphasize this contrast. The speaker has no one to converse with or to enjoy hearing his music or singing.

A tercet is a three-line stanza.

Because I often like to consider the number of lines in my stanzas, I broke them into groupings of two tercets followed by a one-line stanza. By breaking it this way, the poem ended in a manner that separated the last words of the poem into its own short stanza. I did this to demonstrate the isolation further.

Artists' primary audience should be themselves. Writing about our own loneliness, if for no other reason, is good therapy. The intention to share a work should have no bearing on its creation.

Consider this:

At first, the writing may read like a journal, too simple and straight ahead for a poem, because when we're saturated in an emotional low, we aren't often feeling simultaneously analytical and artistic.

> So, it may be that after some *time,*
> we might return to the work to *find*
> an emotional situation that we can *revise*
> (like the *rhyme*
> I
> just worked in there!)

It's in the revisions that we apply our writer's tool kit of literary and poetic devices to craft a presentable work. We may discover some accidently inherent devises in the work like the rhyme I found above. Then, consider what you need to do to accent your discovery.

The Invitation

Write about a time you felt truly lonely. Or, select a particularly prose-sounding example of your journal writing in which you felt lonely. In a revision, consider the reason for your loneliness in that piece, and work it in as a motif.

What contrasts you with the others? Say it clearly. You felt left out for a reason, so don't feel shy to give it voice.

Contrast is an important element in this work. Show your character's situation, and contrast it to the world around. In this example, the speaker's isolation inside the apartment stands in contrast to the neighbor's party. Then, examine your work for poetic devices and literary techniques; use them to emphasize your feelings, and if you don't find many, look for opportunities to add some.

WALKIN' THE TRACKS

I used to walk the tracks for miles.
I got into geology for a while,
and I would examine the rocks I'd find.
"Why this is no rock at all," I'd say. "This is coke from the old coal trains,"
then I'd skip it down the distance.

I could always tell if a track was
used often by the amount of rust on its top.
Home was an open wound, so
I sat under the trestle and waited,
while the train burst rocks or flattened wheat-back pennies
I'd sit upon the track.

It was peaceful out on the gravel flat.
Usually no one else was around,
and that's how I liked it.
Alone, walking plank by plank
down the slow wind of the track,
splitting through the thorny underbrush
like a scar that grows no hair.

The Writer

My grandparents and I lived at the corner of Pine and Yale. There, beyond the dead end, lay train tracks with a trestle and a creek. I spent a lot of time walking both.

I used to flip rocks in the ravine, catch crawdads, or fish for perch; then explore the long bends of the busy tracks.

When the train came, I would sprint down the packed rock, sit beneath the trestle and hang on to a large chunk of scree as the train screamed overhead, its power and noise vibrating through my entire body. It was terrifying and fun.

Later, when my family moved to Lake Dallas, I found another track to walk. It had no trestle, but the coke and stones were fun to hound and throw. Even today, I live by a track, and just as when I was a kid, I can hear a train passing through every night.

Writers often compare trains and time through metaphor. Johnny Cash, for example, did it in the opening lines of "Folsom Prison":

> I hear the train a comin'. It's rolling 'round the bend.
> And I ain't seen the sunshine since I don't know when.
> I'm stuck in Folsom Prison, and time keeps draggin' on.

Our lives, full of memories and baggage, are like trains with many cars. There might be a patina[6] of graffiti, scars and stains, but so long as we don't stall on the crossing, life is good. Allow your scars to fade; you'll be better for it.

For me, it's a Christmas tradition to kill a bottle of whiskey with my step-dad and joke about old times. He cusses me some for who I was and compliments me some for who I am. It's one of the best parts of my Christmas. It's how a family heals.

We mustn't mope about our scars. They make good stories!

---

[6] patina is a thin shiny or dark surface that forms naturally over time, after exposure to the air.

48

The Craft

Setting can serve as an opportunity for indirect characterization. Where our characters choose to go when they choose solitude can tell us more about them.

The dominant image is how the tracks split the underbrush and trees while it bends away in the distance "like a scar that grows no hair." Connecting the tracks to the scar binds the character to the setting. The setting is rugged, lonely and winding, reflecting aspects of the character.

Setting in literature identifies the time, place and mood of a story.

Indirect characterization reveals the personality of a character. This is done through the character's actions and looks, speech, thoughts, and effect on others (how other characters react to this character).

The Invitation

Writing can help us come to terms with our personal histories. Working old wounds through the intellectual rigor of the writing process can help exhaust our interest in dwelling on them. By seeing our thinking on paper, we offer ourselves the hard evidence of whether we have moved past an issue or not. If we haven't, we may discover before it's too late that we died yesterday and have lived life in a wasted ellipsis.[7]

Write about a time you needed solitude. Where did you go? Why did you go there? How did this place reflect how you felt, or what did it say about you at the time?

---

[7] ellipsis is a mark (as ...) indicating an omission (as of words) or a pause.

BETWEEN THE THUMBNAILS OF TWO BUILDINGS

Tar drizzled down the building's edge
like Satan's icing,

molten suffering in a darkness
too horrible to dissipate by daybreak.

A line of dumpsters stinking like the mouths of ignorance
rested along one line of the alley
and the puddled tears of the forsaken lined the other.

And though the coat I wear is my best, as is the suitcase I carry,
it is badly tattered and out of style.
I hate this place,

but I have been judged by my own busted luck,
and I belong here.

I FEEL THE MOON TONIGHT

I feel the moon tonight
living in loops
incredibly scarred and watching
the lively rest from a distance.

I should be like the earth.
We are so much the same
in our properties,
yet I am vacant.

I know the moments when I am red
                    or yellow
                        or blue
                or full and low
                    in the black
some look upon me,
lovers even
and proclaim me beautiful,

but mine are the colors of bruises
and those are the nights the swelling is unbearable
and I linger forward to watch from closer
and though I do not move,
I seem to follow.

The Writer

Depression is usually the last thing most people want to talk about or hear about. So venting in a private notebook can offer great relief.

For some of us, a change in the wind, a dozen phone calls with no friend answering, looking in the pantry or bank account and finding little can wilt us on the couch to silence and staring at a shoe for hours.

Between the Thumbnails of Two Buildings

I had heard about nightmare bosses, but I'd never yet had my turn until a few years back when my immediate appraiser called me in for the "beginning of the year performance conference." At the time, I had the highest scores in the building, so I expected positive feedback. She rated me low.

I felt ambushed. As she spoke, I remember sitting dumbfounded, struggling to make sense of it all. The data was there. I could show it to her, prove I'd done my job, but facts didn't matter. Nine years of superior performance records didn't matter either. Then, it became clear.

I sat back in my chair. "I see what you're doing," I told her. "You're rating me low on the front end, so you can rate me high on the back end and pretend you affected my "improvement." You're using my evaluation as 'evidence' for your own."

Immediately, it became her life's focus to find every flaw, every inconsistency, the smallest infraction and to lean any situation to a negative. It was horrible. She expected me to fold, but she vastly underestimated my capacity to be a complete bastard. I fought. Outwardly, I fought without fear. But inside, I was constantly afraid and filled with stress. I gained weight; my heart enlarged by 10 percent. I became depressed.

Freud said depression is suppressed rage, and in my case, it was true. It felt crushing. In the end, I won, but it was the worst experience of my professional life. I kept my job and transferred to a much better place.

This poem captures a little bit of how trapped I felt. I touch on this experience again in the short story section with "Year of the Rake," where I take revenge in fiction.

I Feel the Moon Tonight
When I'm depressed, I feel like a satellite. Distant. Empty. However, inner darkness is like the night itself; after a time it will pass. To deal with it, I clean or go out to my woodshop and build. Idleness is the waiting trap. I need to be physically busy. So, when I feel it coming on, I know something I've procrastinated doing is about to get done.

The Craft
Both of these pieces illustrate a set-it-up-to-knock-it-down sort of structure. The speakers of each poem narrate a situation; then both poems shift as each speaker comes to their separate revelations.

Between the Thumbnails of Two Buildings
The first three stanzas describe the filthy elements of the alley in metaphor (the set up).

The forth stanza shifts to the speaker, describing him as tonally relative to the alley (the revelation). The speaker resolves that he "belongs" here; this feeling of defeat affirms the depression.

The title suggests that the speaker is being crushed, as one would smash a flea—between the thumbnails—subtly equating him to the vermin.

I Feel the Moon Tonight
This piece takes the common image of the moon in all its colors, size and optical illusion (the set up), then builds a new context to interpret them (the revelation).

The speaker also equates himself to the moon, and then contrasts the moon to the earth.

The Invitation

Write about a time you felt depressed. Divide the poem into a setup and a revelation. You can also take a common thing and reinterpret it, colored with your mood, to mean something unexpected for the reader.

<u>Consider this:</u>

Your depression is still creative energy. It may take time for you to find the distance to stomach working with the writing you create. Nevertheless, here and there a piece will present itself. You'll see a certain turn of situation, a line or two, or something artistic that you can recast from raw personal emotion to material that others will find vivid and accessible.

The muse of depression is a friendly one, but resist writing only when you're depressed. Write regularly to record a variety of emotions and the reasons for them. Try to write every day.

GRAVITY

I woke up drunk on a bench
somewhere
in a flower garden near downtown,
with just a vague relocation
of stumbling
in a random
direction.

I went along the main street
in a general bearing of my apartment, when a car
going the wrong way
smashed into another in the oncoming lane.

Glass showered up, glittering colors in the street lamps,
and the dreams of the dead burst like racing children
into the dark heavens,
and dreams burst from those
and more from those
and dreams were bursting from the foreheads of bursting dreams,
while the glass rained down,
rattling
like spent hourglass sands on the empty a.m. street…

and then the flames.

A SMALL THING

I used to think abortion
was an answer
until
one night
over a prepackaged scampi and cocktail sauce
my second ex-fiancée
told me
pain had hooped her like a crawfish
in the blood-smeared bathtub

blood everywhere
A secret suspected pregnancy
confirmed
when she produced a fetus
no bigger than a shrimp.

Weeping
alone and heart-burst
she cradled
my son
my daughter

dropped it in the water
colored with urine and blood
and flushed it
like a cockroach.

The Writer
Gravity
Composer John Cage called traffic the silence of the city. Traffic is so omnipresent we tune it out; its danger and power are too mundane to notice until we drift, with our own bubble-like frailty, into a lane of fast-moving traffic.

A witness to death, I wondered how many generations were cut short; how many dreams evaporated, with all the swagger of life reduced to so much rubble.

This piece is an amalgam of wrecks I've seen and a bench I may (or may not) have found myself on one night needing to rest while I may (or may not) have been too inebriated to walk home.

A Small Thing
When I was young and in the Army, I remember thinking that if a girlfriend of mine ever became pregnant, no problem! I would pay whatever money to whatever clinic, and whatever.

When it actually happened, and my first ex-fiancée said she was pregnant, and then later lost the baby, I felt horrible. I still feel horrible. I knew then, that for me and mine, abortion disgusted me.

For the world of the poem, I changed her to my "second ex-fiancée" because I thought it sounded more interesting. The change was really just a small thing.

The Craft
Gravity
In addition to its obvious definition, "gravity" can relate to the importance of a situation. Here while havoc rattles down over the spread of wreckage and death, I thought it a good title.

The memorable image of the piece is the dreams of the dead bursting through the foreheads of the dead in perpetuity. It's an image of both the end of life and all the life that could have been.

The flames punctuate the piece—the flame of life devoured by the flames of catastrophe.

A Small Thing

She told me the fetus was "no bigger than a shrimp," and that image has persisted, haunting me. So here, I kept the motif of the fetal curl throughout the poem. In addition, I use the irony of understatement in both the title and the situation to emphasize the impact of the last line.

I wrote her account in a raw matter-of-fact, unblinking manner to convey the stark emotion she and I both felt. I ended the piece, as the moment ended, with no more ceremony than one would flush a bug or a dead goldfish, the vague inference equating death and excrement.

The Invitation

Write about the tragedy you've known. Was this something you witnessed, or was it more personal?

Use your writing about this tragedy to refine your definitions of life's meanings. Examine its irony and unfairness. Consider the boldness with which you describe the situation. If the frankness of your writing feels like you're taking a risk, you may be onto a good poem.

Ask what the memorable image of your piece is, and consider how it furthers the meaning of your work.

IN THE NAME OF LIBERTY

At tax time, the squeegee man at 34th and Antoine
dressed in a gray foam-rubber costume
that looked like Lady Liberty, advertising for a tax preparation
company.

At the curb, splashed by muddy tires striking muddy puddles,
he stood in the Monday drizzle—
a six-foot sponge of dirty rainwater.

Occasionally, by the passersby, he was mocked,
given a drive-through meal, a beer…
some pulled in to tip him for a picture with them.

These days he stood a little taller.
He wasn't working for ashtray change in dark-stained jeans,
and in need of a shave.

He was masked and on the clock for several cash dollars an hour
helping the poor and weary save some money on their returns,
and for a few days, he was a national treasure.

HOGTIED

Somebody told me once I could be anything,
so I wanted to fly.
Pilots look rich
and get to see so much,
but I'm colorblind.
Was denied.

Then I wanted to be a doctor
of some kind
because I dreamed of helping people,
but there's a lot of reading.
I'm dyslexic and could never afford
the tutor.

Politics was out. I have a terrible reputation,
and I can't lie worth a dime.
Being a preacher was impossible because
God has been tied up in a lawsuit
against the U.S. for denying his right to do business...
It'll be a miracle if he wins.

I tried to do
a lot of things
I dreamed about,
and each time
NO
for some good reason.

So I'm left
with what they left me—
wanting,
until I can no longer
even have
that.

Maybe those who told me I could do anything
will rescue me
when I'm flat busted and broken.

Maybe I'll think they're my savior
and love them
like a god.

Maybe that's what they wanted all along.

The Writer

In the Name of Liberty

The squeegee man had an identifiable posture—a hooping of the shoulder. I assume someone from the accounting agency came out and offered him a job. Even through the costume, I could tell it was him. Plus, those were the only days he was "absent" from the corner.

His squeegee always looked bone dry, and I never actually saw him attempt to wash a window. He just held it like it gave him purpose. He didn't even beg, really. He just paced at the easement, and people would call him over occasionally to hand him money or a water bottle. Now and then, he would rave at no one or laugh at something whispered by the concrete.

Once, men in orange vests stood at the red light on his corner collecting money to "help the homeless." He sat in the shadow of the overpass, off to one side—displaced even here. When they brought their jar over to me, I pointedly asked, "What the hell are you doing talking to me, when he's right there needing help?" He replied simply, "You can't help people who don't want it."

"But what if they're too mad to know they want it? He needs medication," I said. They moved on.

Since the writing, he has disappeared. I'd like to imagine that someone helped him, and somewhere is doing better.

Hogtied

With this piece, I'd like to argue that we must accept and forget our shortcomings, only so we may redefine ourselves as those who will succeed—not as downtrodden misfortunates who must be saved. No one will ever save you but you.

Exclusionary stipulations are a sad reality of life. Those who would control us, who would hope to fleece us for their own ends, would like to play on our distresses. They would like to whip us into an outrage about what's fair and what's not. But, for every loser there is a winner, and when the subtext of a situation is that we're the losers, it isn't much of a trick to understand who the winners are supposed to be.

Consider this:

Engage political subjects as you experience them—on a person-to-person level. Ideologues tend to engage their political subjects from issues learned from the media (spun from the media), and it all starts sounding like some Orwellian two minutes of hate[8], "four legs good two legs bad," and blaming Snowball[9] for this and that. If you have a personal story that supports the new, hot media rage, then tell it boldly and let the audience make the connection, or if you think they'll miss it, blend the current event and your story. The result will feel much more powerful than raging about someone else's story in a writing where your personal experience is conspicuously absent.

Also, to write overly political poetry often dates the work—which isn't always bad, just a point to be aware of. Woody Guthrie's poetic songs about Depression-era work camps and his son Arlo Guthrie's Vietnam protest song "Alice's Restaurant" handle the politics beautiful and capture America's cultural milieu. In this spirit, a good political piece serves as a snapshot of ideas circulating at the time.

Overtly political writing may also alienate a portion of the audience or reveal a writer's lack of knowledge on the topic. If you've ever felt put off by a celebrity who has (in your opinion) loony political ideas, you could fall in the same trap so that others in your immediate audience think the same about you.

So, write about what you know. If a political subject interests you that passionately, volunteer for the cause.[10] This is more

---

[8] Two minutes of hate is a period of time in George Orwell's novel *1984* where party members come together to watch a propaganda film and publically express their hatred for the enemy of Oceana (their island society).

[9] Snowball—Based on Leon Trotsky, the character Snowball (a pig) challenges Napoleon (also a pig) for control of Animal Farm in George Orwell's novel *Animal Farm*. "Four legs good two legs bad" is a party slogan that the sheep repeat, and the pigs re-write as they become more human. "Four legs good two legs better!"

[10] In my own experiences I have helped with a gala and art auction for a safe house for victims of human trafficking, and participated in the 100,000 Poets for Change, as well as other fundraisers for the arts.

important than merely talking about it. Don't be a political poet who doesn't volunteer for anything. You'll reduce yourself to merely sounding constantly outraged. Be more than that.

The Craft
In the Name of Liberty
This piece opens with exactly the cross street he stands on. This is so the reader will know the area. We, who live here, know the beggars stand two on every corner.

The crux of the piece is the ironic situation of a social discard disguised as a national symbol, which builds towards the punchline of the work.

The body of the piece is a descriptive list of his various encounters, of which he is always the subject, never in a group or belonging. The only way he participates in even the most superficial, social interactions is by wearing a mask. His mask is a burden; it is a sponge, and he is in the drizzling rain.

Hogtied
The first three stanzas list the dreams and the "but." The fourth stanza begins the realization that expounds throughout the remainder of the poem.

64

The Invitation

Write about something political in nature, but demonstrate your ideas at street level, and relate them through your personal experiences. This will give you credibility as a speaker. A human story is much more interesting to read and is much more easily relatable to our own lives.

What factors have limited your success or excluded you from participating in your various dreams? Let the first stanzas explore what you want. Then, at the shift, meditate on the power exchange due to your exclusion. Who wins and why?

Shift in poetry, also called the turn or the volta, indicates a change in the speaker's understanding, tone, or emotion.

CELLOPHANE VANITY

I had this terrible nightmare
where a rash fell over the horizon
scratched raw by the wine dark sea
The sun rose like an exit song
trying to bud between saloon door clouds
but its shape was wrong
deformed by suffocated rainbows

The people below had become so divorced from the earth
they ridiculed those who posed
proudly in photos with fish they caught or animals they hunted
yet gladly ate those steaks
from the absorbent diaper linings
of yellow Styrofoam
and cellophane packages

They, who spent money for artificially colored, processed foods
genetically engineered and soaked with pesticides
were in their minds superior
to the redneck bumpkins that used skill to join family
and friends on outings in nature
to acquire some of what they ate
They were inferior to those who never left the house or city
but swore they loved the earth

It was a frightening nightmare
that burned from the heavens
to the soil
where irritated redhead grubs twisted, burning, pushing
through the earth
near the succulent roots
of the tomato plant outback

66

The Writer

It's amazing to me how lost we have become that anyone would (of all things) disparage those who take their food from the earth, the most time-honored fulfillment of basic needs that has lasted for the whole of life on Earth. By their actions, these people feel that eating industrial farm-raised, engineered meat off what amounts to a diaper is evolution. It's a snobbery so strange that I can't get my head around it.

This poem is a response to the comments I've heard putting other Americans down. The hyper-political speakers despise anything associated (even stereotypically associated) with the party they hate—hunting and fishing being among these. Yet they eat meat and fish. It seems that, generally, anyone who is a producer—from farmers and ranchers to a number of other blue-collar workers (builders)—are somehow backwards, uneducated and out-of-touch. I think that's ridiculous. Usually, I shy away from political topics, but this time I wanted to respond.

The Craft

I didn't want to call these people out directly, so instead I enter this poem through the idea that my complaint was merely a nightmare, too horrifying to be real.

Since meat is colored red—in this case artificially—I wanted a theme of red in this poem.

The first stanza illustrates the setting: the horizon is a rash; the sun is deformed. The piece is a nightmare, so naturally I wanted to build distorted images. Here too, I echo Homer's description of the ocean as "the wine dark sea," alluding to the *Odyssey*. I could have elaborated bringing in Scylla and Charybdis,[11] but left it out, choosing only to take the color, so not to over-complicate the poem and distract from my central message.

The second and third stanzas detail the hubris and hypocrisy my targets demonstrate while their food is artificially colored,

---

[11] Scylla and Charybdis are two monsters who live across from one another in a narrow channel. They are the "rock and a hard place" Odysseus and his crew must navigate in *The Odyssey*.

preserved, enhanced, etc. In contrast, the redneck bumpkins from "Redneckistan," practicing their "redneckary" join friends, go on outings and eat more naturally.

The final stanza concludes with the earth's discomfort in the nightmare. The earth is burning (which is red), and the image of the red grub resolves with an image of a naturally colored red fruit.

Since I couldn't describe how to hunt engineered food (other than describing a search through bins of cellophane-wrapped packages), I use words like *diaper*, *artificially* and *processed* to create a feeling of disgust. Then I contrast this imagery with the actions of those who use skills, enjoying family and nature, hunting and fishing for natural foods, but are belittled and vilified by those who get their food processed and prepackaged.

The Invitation

Write about a political hypocrisy that has annoyed. If you have a friend or family member who is always talking politics that you don't quite agree with, this might be the perfect chance to set up a nightmare and argue your side.

Don't take on an entire political ideology. Instead, focus on one thing. Draw from your personal experience. Separate the idea from the person and write from your gut. Be visual, and present a clear contrast between your position and theirs.

MY GRAND FINALE

If I am to die in a hospital,
comfortable in an automatic adjustable bed,
having escaped my youth in one piece,
I will take a pen to capture my final thoughts.
Make my last poems,
so you can know,
until my thin, liver-spotted hands
are too weak to write.

Then, I will have a recorder placed near my lips
so I can whisper rhyme,
speak in clever rhythms,
          creating just a few more
poems before it is time,
until I am too weak to speak.

Then I will lie still,
thinking . . .

And, the last few
poems I make,
before this body pushes me out,
I will keep for myself.

A MOMENT OF PEACE

When I lie down
after mixing pills and whisky,
acid burns in my throat, making it hard to sleep.
So, with eyes closed, I remember moments
from years past,
recreate a smile,
smell, conversation.

I see grandmother's kitchen, her small wood table,
centerpiece of plastic grapes, a pear, red apple.
They were hollow and never dusty.

I remember afternoons in a pecan tree, looking out over the busy
street,
watching automobiles crash at the intersection,
or when the Doberman
jumped from an old Chevy, dangling
from its harness-leash, until it was helped
—yelping in terror—back into the bed.

I remember a girl I loved.
Holding her while she slept,
and laughing.
          We laughed a lot before the end.

On rare times, I run in a big yard
playing in the evening light with old dogs I've had—
different ones that were stolen, lost, killed, or distempered.
I wonder if they wait in heaven with my grandparents,
or if there is a heaven . . .
I imagine people I could meet
if I make it there.

Then finally, memories mingle
with the pills and the whisky, the acid and the dreams.

The Writer

My Grand Finale

A reckless life builds insipidly. Eating badly. Drinking excessively. Living dangerously. They all set up ambush positions until one day a whole hairball of health problems unravels, and it's lights out. However, knowing that doesn't get me back to the gym or make me say, "I'll be passing on that pie today."

If I'm honest, even the death of someone close or discovering a health issue only straightens me up for a short while.

It's only through writing that I build my own little pyramid—a monument that I won't be buried in, that my life is coded through, that will stand beyond my years (even if for a short while).

A Moment of Peace

Art is the perspiration of pain. Creative people think deeply, and though externally we may appear stoic, we feel deeply, too. It is only natural that we would contemplate the afterlife and our worthiness. I remember not liking myself very much, as a kid. I would lie in bed wondering if I deserved to go to Heaven, and settling on—probably not.

The Craft

My Grand Finale

This piece is a deductive structure that moves from the character feeling weak, to weaker, to death.

The poem resolves recognizing the idea that our death is the most intensely personal process we will go through (besides our birth), and we take that last little bit of knowing about the other side with us, uncommunicated to the outside world.

A Moment of Peace

One way your character might discover something surprising about himself is to create several seemingly unrelated moments tethered beneath a single theme, as I have done in "A Moment of Peace," in which the character is abusing himself and recalls the more wholesome moments of his youth.

The Invitation

Write while contemplating your own mortality or worthiness.

Consider the scope in which you present your ideas: do you move from general to specific, specific to general, or did you forget to consider that at all? Thinking about this can bring order and flow into your work.

Mechanism

LITURGY OF A HOLY ROCK AND ROLL POET

I threw my empty across the room to the trash pile
and sat back on the little couch. A few friends were over
and had questions. They were poor too
but somehow figured I held a key, something magic that would one day
move me uptown. They listened, and this is what I told them:

> We all drink, sing,
> smoke and dream,
> but dreams are empty pockets
> if dream is all you do,
> and you'll wind up
> like nearly everybody else;
> a could've been,
> a common man.
>
> Of course, there's nothing wrong with that,
> if you don't think anything is.
>
> It takes more to *hustle* ambition,
> persevering through the process:
> Lonely nights, block and rewrites.
> Peddling yourself to agents, publishers and living
> the drunken misery of it all.
> But there are a few who endure
> and when the dust settles,
> they are achievers.
>
> That's the difference in feeling like a winner
> or a loser.
> Achievers have all been dreamers

dreams are the easy part.

If you don't mind regret,
or being a failure for lack of trying,
then I guess it's okay for you
to stop there.

Now put on a record and
pass me another beer.

They did, and I drank it.

LECTURE OF SOUL

I awoke with my soul in a cockroach
standing like Father Time on a bag of rice
in a cabinet over the oven.
He wore a monocle on a gold chain,
spoke eloquently with great manners,
aside from the fact he was stealing my rice.

He cleared his throat and said:

> "Refine your philosophy,
> defy temptation.
> Indulge in thought
> and constructive recreation.
>
> Leave emotion to the ocean tempest
> swallowed without line,
> without direction
> until you fish from the brine
> a beauty perfect to plant your affections.
>
> Then, quell the swells and strive.
> Strive for strength together.
> Fight at length
> to love her.
>
> Love her forever
>
> and know life
> from the death
> you had before!"

With a napkin, I crushed him in a fist.
Lightning fast!
He never had a chance.
I never wanted him to have a chance.

He was a thief.

I always hated thieves.

I stole back my soul, rice, his words and advice,

then flushed him where all thieves belong,
considering his words,
while he twisted down the pipe.

The Writer

Liturgy of a Holy Rock and Roll Poet

When I got out of the army, I moved into a low-income housing unit in Lewisville, Texas. There were four units upstairs and four units downstairs. Each floor had two doors dead ahead, one left and one right. Mine was upstairs immediately on the right. Living there, I had three things I knew I could count on: roaches, some kind of violence and drugs.

Somehow, I landed right in the cookie jar. The people living in the two units forward of the staircase sold cocaine and crank, and the guy immediately on the left dealt marijuana. However, I was fresh from the service, and I had no interest.

At the time, all I owned in the world was a guitar and a duffel bag. I walked through the door completely moved in, and the apartment was still completely empty. Over the next weeks, I watched the dumpster, and ran out to gather furniture, silverware, a towel and, finally, a bed with sheets.

Since I had the guitar, my neighbors and some of the regular traffic that passed through would congregate at my house. They brought me food and asked my advice on things, but in many ways, they were actually better off than me. At least they had some dishes.

Lecture of Soul

The body of this piece began as disembodied advice to myself jotted in the pages of a journal. I culled it from a notebook one night while looking for surrealistic pieces to include in a collection I wrote called *Thirsty Earth*. I knew I could sandwich setting around the rant to make it work.

That morning, I'd gone to my cabinet for something to eat and saw a roach so big on my sack of rice, I could tell it was male. Our eyes locked in a stare-down like Old West gunslingers. The world stopped except for a tiny dust ball tumbleweed near the fridge that somersaulted by. Each of us knew one would die.

He fought well—making a wild leap at my face. But, what can I say? The better man won.

80

The idea of metempsychosis is the soul shifting into another person or animal. I had Yeats' "A Dialogue of Soul and Self" in mind before my duel.

The Craft
Liturgy of a Holy Rock and Roll Poet
This piece comes from a journal entry inspired after one night with my neighbors. I had many journal entries like this: conversational with no real setting, conflict, with no backdrop for the words to happen around.

On its face, the piece was rather preachy and uninteresting. Call it lipstick on a pig, but I sandwiched the preachy bit between descriptions of a situation to brighten it up with some of the elements it had been missing.

Lecture of Soul
I wanted to connect the formless voice with characters and setting. Disembodied from the setting, I thought the writing sounded silly by itself. Therefore, I wanted the cockroach's speech to come across as a sad attempt to misdirect the man's attention while he stole the man's rice. But the man could never fall for the melodramatic, pedestrian sounding advice. He kills the roach, yet still considers the meaning in its words.

Once again, as with "Liturgy," I began with a "preachy" sort of journal piece and tried to salvage it by connecting it to character and setting. Of the two pieces, I believe "Lecture of Soul" is more successful. I think the humor carries it, but maybe I just like seeing a low-down-dirty thief get his comeuppance.

The Invitation
Write using setting as a mechanism. Find preachy, lecture-style samples of your writing and give them setting and characters.

Keep in mind, there is a great difference between a work written for personal therapy (intended for just ourselves, private) and work written as art (intended for an audience).

Therapeutic pieces tend to sound so intensely personal that they are often rather impenetrable or trite. They frequently brim so fully with self-pity, self-recriminations, emotional assaults on God, family, politics, or whatever that the audience has heard so many times before it bores them. Through their own polite determination, an audience will usually sit and take it, then affirm the reader's effort with a conciliatory applause that speaks more to their own home training than it complements the work. Beware of this.

Consider this:

One evening after my victory over the cockroach, while fashionably smug, I reclined on my sofa reading Japanese philosophy. Tetsuro Watsuji in his book *Rinrigaku* said something I found quite liberating as a writer. He argued that individuality was a myth. Uniqueness was also a myth because society has coerced everything upon us—from our language to what we find acceptable and unacceptable, attractive and unattractive. Even when we rebel, it's normal.

With seven billion people on the planet, the likelihood of being unique or saying something new is slim.

The second-century philosopher Horace noticed this as well when he wrote, "It has all been said." At the time, the world population was around 200 million. We can imagine it has been said quite a few times by now.

Writers know this, but we continue to write because readers don't say, "Tell me about you, oh interesting writer. Tell me how unique and exclusive your life has been. Enlighten us about your unfathomable existence which we could never understand!" In fact, it's the complete opposite of this. Readers feel insulted when writers are so self-involved.

All a reader actually says is "Tell me about me. Validate an experience I've had, or create something for me to experience vicariously, so that I may develop and exercise my empathy."

Good writers do this with truth and fiction, or both at the same time, hiding truth in fiction.

Knowing this, you can talk about the intimacy of your life in an open, accessible way that assumes the reader can connect. Celebrate your lack of uniqueness. Write honestly (or at least with the feeling of honesty), and readers will naturally relate.

AND JESUS SAID, "CHOP WOOD AND I AM THERE."

Sitting on a broken piece of concrete,
I'm looking down on the Corpus Christi landfill.
Great aluminum tires roll bulldozers over collapsed
milk jugs, diapers and paper.

Laughing gulls pick through the diapers,
boxes and tall white kitchen bags
looking for anything.

There is a mesquite tree close enough
that I lean back on it, watching
the methane stream from the long
domino lines of gray metal pipes.

This is a place people don't usually come to.
There are no horns to honk,
teenagers to roll their eyes,
administrators to lecture,
or rude store clerks here.

So I come to listen
to the hissing pipe organ of methane,
choir of gulls,
and dozers droning long sermons
from mountaintops of garbage.

In the soft rays of the evening
relaxing beneath thorny limbs
and a vista that's as condemned as the garbage in it,
I find peace from the world
and claim a little piece of heaven for myself.

The Writer

I don't remember why I went to the landfill that day—probably helping someone for a side job. However, the science there fascinated me. The methane, the layers of clay lining the pit, the huge, studded aluminum tires on the bulldozers.

Seagulls laughed and leapt in huge white flocks; it looked like a shot from a PBS episode panning over millions of flamingos. It was hard to tell the flutter of their wings from the tumbling plastic grocery sacks flowing in the bulldozer's wake.

On the ridge, along the top edge of the pit, ran a tall fence lining the landfill, but right behind that stood a shady mesquite grove. Though I didn't get to go up, I imagined what it might feel like resting there, unbothered, watching the activity of the fill.

The title comes from saying 77b in the Gospel of Thomas:[12] "Jesus said, 'I am the light that is over all things. I am all: from me all came forth, and to me all attained. Split a piece of wood; I am there. Lift up the stone, and you will find me there.'"

The Craft

Impressed by the irony of my feelings, I kept that contrast throughout the piece. Juxtaposing something unclean with something discussed in holy terms. By choosing words that typically describe, or suggest, church, I have built and superimposed a motif of church over the setting of a landfill. I define the gulls, which are cacophonous and loud, as a choir,

> Juxtapose—setting two unalike things in a scene to contrast one another for artistic statement.

the steaming pipes as a pipe organ, etc. Collectively these make the basic argument that church, in some form, is where you make it.

---

[12] The Gospel of Thomas is an early Christian non-canonical sayings gospel composed of 144 says attributed to Jesus Christ.

Consider also that this is how we extend metaphor. This kind of motif and irony helps the poet show what's common in a new light.

> Extended metaphor is a metaphor that has been introduced and developed throughout all or part the literary work.

The Invitation

Write using the setting ironically. Have you found peace, or enjoyment, in a place that others shun?

Consider what connotations about that setting you want readers to have, then brainstorm items that commonly bring to mind those associations and blend them with your narrative to build motif.

Evaluate the quality of your metaphor and the tension it builds. Do your metaphors build in terms of the subject? For example, if the writing is about baseball, do you use baseball metaphors? If the piece is about the ocean, do your metaphors lend themselves to that?

Is the playroom a circus, a natural disaster, a mortuary? Is it a glossy swarm of tumbled yellow and red, or do you build tension by describing it in terms of a military graveyard, precisely set and grayed with the whispered notes of "Taps"? In a different vein, is your boss's face like a skillet that has fried too many turkey necks, his nose a bulbous gobbler flopped over his lip like an old tom turkey that's too crippled and worthless for slaughter? Of course it isn't! That would be mean.

What Do You Read, My Lord?

I will never write a poem
about my love of words—
how they inspire and
move and validate and
communicate
my heart, my mind,
my immortal and tender
weeping soul—the soul
I've never met
that is somewhere on the
ledge of
a chiasmus

Sitting at the seashore
watching the sun set,
shoring what it sees with
no son sitting next to it.
In the wild wind of winding words
washing in the surf,
giving birth
to those feral
unbridled,
majestic
piebald mustangs of
language!

Words words words that
aren't "its" but "whos."
Words with their own
brawn and savoir faire
Words who can both woo
a woman
and drag a man out back
to dash his brains
against their wit all in the
same whisper...

Oh, by all the Saints who
ever lived

and were rumored to live,
I will never write about
how words
saved my miserable life
and how I was destined
to be
something awful and devilish
if they weren't my outlet,
my toil,
and the reason for my
vast collection of blunted
pencils
with no erasers, time-hardened erasers,
extra aftermarket erasers
with the tops worn
through so that just a
collar
of eraser hangs on its
metal neck
like quitter sock... no, like
a shackle!
Bound to the page,
a slave to words, words,
words.

Oh, no, that's such a
dumb poem to write.
And I never write dumb
poems.

The Writer

I've always found it incredibly corny when poets write about their "love" of words. It tops my groan meter with "I cried when I wrote this," as well as any poem that begins in performance with the poet yelling while poppin' and lockin' overly choreographed movements. It comes off as hyperbolic, sappy and funny (though rarely intended to be). They make me laugh, so my response has to be humorous.

In Act II, Scene 2 of *Hamlet*, Polonius asks Hamlet, "What do you read, my lord?" and Hamlet replies, "Words, words, words." I knew that would be my platform.

In Act III, Scene 2, Shakespeare offers his only advice for acting (which we can also apply to writing and poetry performance). Prince Hamlet tells the actors how he wants the lines of his play delivered. He says, "Do not saw the air too much with your hand, thus, but use it all gently." Then a few lines down he says, "suit the action to the word, the word to the action, with special observance that you o'erstep not the modesty of nature. Make it as life."

Since poems about a writer's love of words are so rarely like life, I thought it would be funny to metaphorically saw the air too much with my hand, be completely unlike life and ostensibly ignore all of Hamlet's advice while alluding to his line, "Words, words, words." Then in a further irony, accidently write a poem exactly on the topic I'm swearing to never write.

The Craft

A chiasmus is a text structure that doubles back on itself as seen in the line from Rogers and Hammerstein's famous musical *Cinderella*: "Do I love you because you're beautiful, or are you beautiful because I love you?" It is also, of course, here in *Hamlet* when Hamlet says, "Suit the action to the word, the word to the action . . ."

To further the idea of chiasmus, I rave against the idea of writing about

Chiasmus is a Latin term from the Greek meaning "crossing." Chi is the Greek letter X.

one's love of words, then ironically turn back around and do so. To make the chiasmus even more ridiculous, I bend the homonyms, heterographs and heteronyms then let it all race together with abundant alliteration.

While writing, I decided that "piebald" sounded unusual and funny, so I wanted it in there, connected to the completely clichéd image of wild horses picturesquely splashing through the surf.

Blissful ignorance is another great comedic tool. When you create characters who are oblivious to their own circular logic, hypocrisy and even stupidity, you let your readers feel superior while they remain sympathetic and even laugh at themselves if they relate (as poets might who have also held up their poetry like Yorick's skull and written about their love of words).

The Invitation

Write about what you think is overdone in writing (overly erotic sex, politics, angry at Dad, God, the president, the media, *Twilight*-style vampires, derogatory songs, the beauty of nature, love, etc.). Make a clear statement, swearing that you would never write about it. Overuse a few poetic devises, be hyperbolic and blissfully ignorant to the notion that you're doing exactly what you said you wouldn't. And profess it as if you mean it.

Homonyms are words that have the same spelling and pronunciation but different meanings, such as shore (noun, land along the edge of water) and shore (verb, to prop up). Heterographs are words that have the same pronunciation but different meaning and spelling, such as sun (the star of our solar system) and son (a male child). Heteronyms are words that have the same spelling but have different meaning and pronunciation, such as wind (noun, breeze) and wind (verb, twist).

Alliteration is the repetition of initial sounds, usually a consonant, in a group of words next to or near each other, such as Peter Piper, leaping lizards, and Betty's banter did not bother Bobby. Contrast this with consonance and assonance which occur within the words such as the "r" sound in Peter Piper, and the "e" sound in "Peter, Betty's."

Clichéd is an adjective meaning trite and unoriginal.

Almost Tender

Her gold nugget eyes shine from the green river's edge,
silent and lethargic.
Huge cone-like teeth protrude without gums
without mercy,
capable of one thousand pounds of pressure per square inch.

Last month she took a possum right off his limb
like picking fruit from an overhanging branch
but just now,
in her savage mouth
she cradles the tiny bodies of her chirping young.

The Writer

Some of my favorite nature documentaries focus on big predators. I'd never seen an alligator in real life until I went fishing in Lake Livingston near a boat ramp, having no luck. Nothing was biting. A six-foot alligator patrolled near and far from where I stood. His eyes swept over me; my eyes swept over him. Our eyes met like intersecting searchlights. I knew much bigger gators lurked nearby.

Darkness dropped. I had worked down to fish the slips—still nothing. I went back to the spot I'd fished before, cautiously watching for the alligator. They're an ambush predator, but so am I. I steeled myself and neared the bank. As I went to cast, something exploded in a rush from the tree line—a deer with its belly swollen.

Processing the shock of the moment, the strange, distended belly of the pregnant deer and feeling certain a giant demonic alligator had ambushed me, I prepared for the death roll! It startled me half to death. Luckily, there was no gator, and I lived to fish another day. And the fish, who have brains so small they may not actually have any brains, continue to outsmart me.

As strikingly rugged as alligators are, it's interesting how they exhibit such tenderness to their newborn young.

The Craft

I focus on the eyes and teeth to depict the alligator as dangerous and powerful. Then I confirm those images with an action and end the piece using situational irony to demonstrate the animal in a different light, using contrasting words like "savage" and "cradle."

Irony turns the description into a poem.

Situational irony occurs when actions have the exact opposite effect of what was intended, and the outcome is contrary to what was expected.

The Invitation

Write using situational irony. Establish something common; then reveal an unexpected or insightful aspect to it. Draw on your own experiences in nature, or recall something interesting from a documentary or another work.

If you do it in two quatrains like I did, use one to set up the situation and the next to release the irony.

A quatrain is a four-line poem or stanza.

LITTLE JACK FRAZZLE

Little Jack Frazzle
just loved to dazzle
his friends by walking the wire
that their applause
had somehow caused
to work itself higher and higher.

Well, one day he tripped
from the wire he slipped
and landed flat on his face.
His friends they were rotten
and with Jack soon forgotten
found how easy he was to replace.

COFFEE AND SCONES

Stoned to the bone
on coffee and scones
while the lecturer's lecture
drones and drones,

the crowd is on their laptops
and texting on their phones.

The Writer
Jack Frazzle
Running around, trying to please schoolmates with my antics was never my style as a kid. However, from the wings, I watched as other children did. They let the "in crowd" dare them and pressure them into making fools of themselves. Then as soon as they got hurt or fell out of grace, another idiot lined up.

Our memories are fantastic white-washers of the past. Our writing is a time capsule of our emotions and opinions captured in a snapshot. I wrote this poem at 16 years old, after seeing the behavior firsthand.

Coffee and Scones
Spiral-eyed and numb, I've suffered through many, horrible meetings, and with the other participants shuffled around for whatever excuse I could find: a pastry, the restroom, pecking at a laptop—anything to burn so-slow hours, while the panes of windows seem to thicken at the bottoms until at last sweet relief! Parole! We win release from the droning boredom of a compulsory presentation, administered by a drone who felt as lousy giving it as we did receiving it.

Didactic—writing that is intended to teach.

Explicit theme—a theme that is clearly stated.

Add these meetings to the list of death and taxes as something we all have to endure.

The Craft
Generally didactic in nature with an explicit theme, nursery rhymes offer writers the chance to play with driving rhythm while embedding life lessons in their work.

In other incarnations, Jack has gone up the hill, up the beanstalk, been nimble and quick, last name Frost, last name Spratt, last name Horner and O'Lantern. This time Jack wears the last name Frazzle, as he is quite frazzled with how he allows others to use him.

Jack Frazzle

The poem is in two stanzas. The first stanza is the situation before the fall. The second stanza is the situation after the fall and contains the takeaway lesson of the piece.

Coffee and Scones

Nursery rhymes don't have to be childish. You can talk about your daily life while keeping the same fun, driving rhythm and meter.

In addition, writing them looks as if you're taking notes and listening intently to the boss at his super-ultra-important-informative-very-necessary meetings! Let the off-task workers be obvious and whisper. You're focused! (On writing).

Rhythm is the pattern of stressed and unstressed syllables in a line of verse. In speech this is natural.

The Invitation

Write a short nursery rhyme with a simple situation and an obvious lesson. Imagine the sound of a running horse (clip-clop, clip-clop) and write to that rhythm.

Meter, meaning measure in Greek, is a premeasured pattern of stressed and unstressed syllables. These units of collected patterns, when considered individually, are called poetic feet. Pentameter, for example, is a line of five (penta-) metric feet.

Consider what it is that you would like to teach. Is it manners, the importance of

Hyperbole is an exaggerated statement or claim not meant to be taken literally.

education, proper interpersonal relations, proper spelling or respect for other people's property? What does the next generation need to know, and what's a fun, imaginative way to tell it to them?

Use hyperbole and irony as I did or experiment with different poetic devises.

THE EXTENDED METAPHOR OF A LAZY MAN

Dirty clothes lay all over the house
like autumn leaves,
brightly colored
in rustling heaps
deep on city streets,

where traffic twists them up
into the air and over one another
in somersaulting waves,
where they are constantly revealing
and obscuring one another,
diminishing each time,

until the once fine pallet of color
is a filthy sludge of stinking refuse,
until my drawers are empty as barren limbs
scratching at the bitter midnight,
and it is laundry day again.

VESSELS

Is this love a crack in my favorite drinking jar?
Did we mix it all
a bit too tall

tip it back too fast
and dash it to the tabletop forgetting
it was made of glass?

HOARFROST

In the dim shadows of our pride
we pass great souls, spirits that
would light the drafty castles of our lives.

We smile, nod, while the heels of our
shoes click by and fade to distance.

At end, so many of us are alone
because we lacked the desperate courage
to say "*hello.*"

The Writer

The Extended Metaphor of a Lazy Man

Living in a third-story apartment, I had to lug all my clothes down flight after flight, then across and around the parking lot to the mat, only to wait in line, get my clothes stolen if I left them unattended and have bleach spots mysteriously appear on my few good clothes. I put off laundry day until I couldn't any longer.

Instead of "Bounty-fresh," I settled for "That doesn't stink too bad."

However, I have reformed! I own a washer and dryer now and have a wonderful housekeeper. I skip three meals a month to pay for her, but she is better than food. Best money I ever spent beyond my means! Life is good, and I have clean clothes. (Lazy men must abide!)

Vessels

When my second ex-fiancée—or was it my third?— and I were calling it quits, I used to love drinking out of a one quart Ball jar with a handle on the side. As I sat it down one day, I noticed a star-shaped crack in the bottom. My favorite drinking glass was broken!

That had to be some kind of low. I lost my favorite lady and my favorite drinking jar both in the same night.

Hoarfrost

Dostoyevsky used the metaphor of comparing our lives to castles. I thought it so brilliant, I wanted to allude to him and try out the concept for myself.

I've wondered how many of us pass someone attractive who is also lonely and continue forward only to nod politely, too busy and too shy for love.

To title the piece, I considered this: hoarfrost is the gray frost of morning, and it's the graying hair on the sides of the head. The word "hoary" means stale, worn, or worn-out. I thought of the gray stones of a castle, the frost of loneliness, our own aging.

The Craft
Consider this:

The basic structure of a simile is that Object B tells us more about Object A.

> Ex: She (object A) is growing like a weed (Object B).
> Weeds grow quickly; therefore, she is growing fast.

Metaphors are condensed similes. However, they don't directly translate. We will not get the same effect saying, "She (Object A) is a growing weed (Object B)."

That sounds insulting and is not the intended message.

However, if we say, "The road was a ribbon of moonlight" as Alfred Noyes writes in his famous poem "The Highwayman," we know: the road (Object A) is a ribbon (Object B).

Ribbons are thin and winding, therefore the road is thin and winding. Made of moonlight, the road is barely lit, so it's also dangerous.

An extended metaphor or extended simile continues to add information, building a motif as it extends or unpacks.

The Extended Metaphor of a Lazy Man

I used to wear a variety of colors. Heaped together in the laundry sack, they looked like autumn leaves in a trash bag, plenty faded and old, and probably not far from the actual trash sack (or rag drawer).

Of my three examples, this is the longest, yet it's only one sentence long.

Vessels

This poem is set up in two tercets (three line stanzas) with two of the three lines rhyming. The first question sets the problem. The second question elaborates as it defines.

This poem's shift is an example of one that amplifies rather than refutes what has come before.

Hoarfrost

The entirety of the first stanza (all three tiny lines) is the first sentence. It defines the guiding metaphor. The second and third stanzas elaborate on that definition, extending the metaphor.

The asyndeton in the second stanza serves to slow the pace of the reading, emphasizing the focus on the sound of the shoes.

Asyndeton is the purposeful omission of coordinate conjunctions (for, and, nor, but, or, yet, so) for syntactical effect. Contrast to polysyndeton, which is the purposeful addition of conjunctions for syntactical effect.

When we only have one or two devices in a poem, we want to use syntactical structures to turn the reader's attention in their direction.

The Invitation

Write a poem that's an extended metaphor. Use my sentence structure if it's helpful. Begin with a metaphor or simile, and keep it going. Let the first stanza set up the situation. Try to use a moment from your life. Then begin adding new aspects, images or problems while keeping the same motif. Let it unpack.

THE WEEPING WILLOW

What's so sad to make the weeping willow weep?
What strange and subtle secret does the willow keep?

I fear that Mother Nature meant we should never know
Why she cursed this timid tree to weeping as she grows.

The Writer

When I was a kid, I cut grass for money to buy books. I would read these books like treasures, hardly opening them to avoid damaging the spines. One day, while cutting around a willow tree, I began to consider its name. I understood the literal sense of the name, of course. It's named for its limbs that weep downwards. But in the fantasy sense of the name, I began to wonder what could have caused it such sorrow that it should weep for all time.

The Craft

This is a simple rhyme in two couplets. The first couplet poses the question. The second couplet offers the resolution.

I composed and memorized this simple piece as I worked. I like manual labor because it gives me time to think. Plus, no one bothers a guy working. They're too worried he might ask for help!

Consider this:

Not all prewriting happens on the page. We actually do a great deal of our planning in the mind. For me, it's only when I might forget, if I've hit a wall or if the scope of the project is too broad and complicated that I need to map it out.

If prewriting feels like an extra, unnecessary step then—in that situation— it probably is. Prewriting is a tool. Tools are useful. Use prewriting techniques when they are helpfully productive, and don't use them when they are not.

Free writing, webbing, clustering and outlining are some of the most common forms of prewriting.

Free writing is a one-person brainstorming activity (brainstorming, as it's commonly known is actually supposed to be a group activity; if done by a single person, it's called listing). Many nights of regular writing begin with this one. Often there's no subject in mind until the pen starts moving. Some writers like to time this activity, such as 15 minutes or whatever. I do not. I just write. Some nights this is a journal entry. Other nights, I'll earn a poem.

Webbing is the prewriting process of mapping thoughts, which branch from a central idea. Lines collect and link these thoughts as they expand outward from the center. Use this when ideas come so quickly you will forget them (or their relationship to one another) if you try to write them in an orderly fashion. I use this one for larger projects.

If you have many notes on many scraps, and they become hard to keep track of, you will want to *cluster* your notes at some point to begin making order of them. This is done (obviously) by putting similar ideas, subjects, and what-have-you together. When writing novels or longer short stories, I end up with notes on all kinds of papers, out of all kinds of notebooks. I scrapbook these all into a single composition book and dictate these into a voice-to-text program (for speed) to manipulate them into an outline form.

Outlining is a useful technique for showing the major and minor relationships between ideas. This is effective when collating into sequential order the material harvested from webbing, free writing, lists and clusters.

The Invitation

Write literally interpreting a metaphor. Take a common name from nature, and write a piece wondering about how they received their names. Is the monarch butterfly a benevolent leader? Is the sand lion king of the sand? What cowboy rides a mustang grape? Consider names like cottonwood tree, wildflower, black-eyed Susan, bullfrog, etc. and offer attributes or histories that confirm or disprove the accuracy of the name.

Does the world have them all wrong, or do we have them pegged perfectly?

SURVIVING THE FLOOD

From atop Cemetery Hill
we watched Lake Lewisville
exhale beyond its banks
pushing gray drift logs, dead stands and litter

past the point of good fishing
crossing the street, white rapids in the ditch, over my lawn,
sweeping off my garden gnome,
then our trailer like a breaching whale rolled sideways through the
yard.

Who knew the dead, like moles, had tunneled to freedom
hoping for a day like this
until the cemetery hillside crumbled and the caskets floated out into
the flotsam
joining in the bumping, churning orgy of the storm.

Finally, once everything was smashed, scatted and half-buried
beneath the slit and debris,
I saw the remnant of my chain-link fence, woven through by
misfortune's hand
with grasses, Styrofoam coolers and broken wood.

A condom, half out-turned and well stretched, drooped from a stick
planted in my front yard like the storm's victory flag
half-flapping in the wind.

And as I surveyed the mess
of what used to be mine, I thought,
"That's about right."

The Eggs are Burning

The eggs are burning.
I kiss her good morning to wake her,
and she tells me that in her dream
a secret only meant for her was being
whispered, and now she'll never know it.

I snuggle up close, but the side of her neck
is all cinched up.
"I don't want to kiss you," she says.

The eggs are burning.
My suitcase fell over.
Her eyes drifted to it,
and that was the first time she smiled all morning.

The Writer
Surviving the Flood

This piece is a good example of autobiographical fiction. Several true-life episodes blend with fiction to create the truth of the piece.

Here's the truth:

My trailer park dead-ended into a graveyard, which wasn't exactly the picture of hope. I heard a saying from someone I've long forgotten: "You live in a box; you drive in a box; and when you die, you're buried in a box." I thought about that every day I passed that cemetery until the day someone a few trailers down ate one of the peacocks that roamed the area, then I thought about that for a while. I bet that peacock tasted delicious!

A knotted sock plugged a hole in my bedroom floor that kept the mice out. Ants ran freely through the house. My bedroom window leaked, and I think the hallway floor caved in once, but luckily, our trailer never actually washed out in a flood. That did happen, though, to other people who lived not so far away and were in my same situation.

In the late 1990s, Texas had some devastating floods. Swisher Cemetery is, in fact, quite flat, so through the rain, it held. However, in other parts of the state, cemetery hills failed, and the dead belched up and washed out for a final escapade through the churning streets.

I connected this to a memory from when I was much younger living in Tulsa, Oklahoma. We'd had many days of rain, and a used condom washed into that backyard of our duplex.

I stood in a puddle arguing with my friend Darren about who would hop the fence for our whiffle ball. The neighbor fought pit bulls, which were quite dangerous, so whoever it was had to be quick!

But Darren spied the condom and being a rather sheltered lad, he had his hands on it filling it at the spigot like a water balloon before I could yell out, in a persuasive format, a science lesson explaining that he might like to drop that, as it was no balloon. Something boiled out, and in a hail of curses, he dropped it and sloshed back a few paces. Telling him he was too dumb to survive the fetching, I darted through the mud and water after the ball. The dog got after me, but I was too quick.

That triggered the memory of walking to my apartment years later and seeing a different (presumably) used condom carried up with other debris in a dust devil. To date that is the most safety conscious dust devil I've ever seen.

These memories, and fragments of memories, were the elements I began with. I didn't have them preordered; they ordered themselves as I wrote. The same diffuse thread I used to make metaphor also fetches and connects memory parts like these.

So blending truth, my fears, current events and memories all into a short piece, I described my feelings on life at the time.

So is the piece true? A court of law would prove that the poem is not true. Nevertheless, insofar as it accurately communicates my real feelings at the time through metaphor and narrative, it is exactly true.

In this spirit, we can see how the presence of truth in literature doesn't necessarily depend on something having actually happened.

The Eggs Are Burning

My third ex-fiancée and I weren't doing well. I wanted to surprise her with breakfast, but as all things go at the end, this turned out like my cooking. Badly.

This poem happened exactly as I wrote it. Right after she smiled about my suitcase falling over, I reached onto the nightstand, popped open my journal and wrote this down while sitting next to her.

The Craft

Surviving the Flood

The poem begins by setting the scene of the flood. From the cemetery, we could stand and see the spot where we used to fish from the bridge. When the lake flooded, that area washed over, and the water started creeping up the street but stopped well before it got to us.

In my writing, though, I brought the water on through. The next stanza is that description. I also never owned a garden gnome. I've never liked them, so I gladly swept it off in a flood.

The third stanza shifts to a new topic with a rhetorical question. I didn't punctuate it with a question mark though. I liked it punctuated with a period, to sound more declarative.

The fourth stanza brings the speaker back to the remnants of his home to process what had just happened.

I ended with an image of a stick caught in the debris. The mention of the condom is surprising in the poem. An inference is a between-the-line reading. Therefore, assuming that everyone understands the purpose of a condom, and considering that anyone who has lost everything in a flood might feel a little screwed by the storm, the inference works. The image may also bring up other issues to the reader's mind, so for that reason, I chose to leave it hanging there with all those issues unaddressed, except for saying: That's about right.

You must learn to work with the power of inference in writing. It allows authors to leave a gap through which readers can participate. It invites reader-response criticism (which proposes that readers co-create meaning with writers) and allows for corrigibility (each reader seeing something slightly different).

The Eggs Are Burning

A little know-how can turn good eggs into great eggs. The same might be said with love. I apparently do not have that know-how, and by the way, my eggs are lousy, too.

This piece opens with the urgency of food burning. The male character is presumably doing the cooking. He only has one other action in the piece: he tries to kiss her good morning. And though he is trying to be thoughtful, he has interrupted a dream in which the female character was learning something important. He ruined that moment, and now she will never know it. Therefore, he is both rejected and rebuffed. In short, he gets "burned."

I use the refrain "The eggs are burning" as my transition between movements. The first is a description of their interaction; the second scene is the falling suitcase and her smile.

The crux of the piece is in the reader's inferred meaning of *his* suitcase falling over. The effect would have felt slightly different had it been her suitcase. However, since his suitcase is the one in motion, we infer that she imagines him leaving. Consider how less effective it would have been if I had her say outright, "What if you left?"

The Invitation

Write experimenting with the power of inference. Give the audience the between-the-lines clues without spelling it out. Children's author Jean Craighead George once said, "Never underestimate the intelligence of your audience." That should be a liberating concept. As writers, we do not need to over-explain ourselves. It's often more powerful to allude to common things rather than obviously spelling them out. Your audience will know what you're driving at.

Poetry has something to do with being distilled, concentrated, compacted. The power of inference will assist with achieving this.

Try a brief poem with two scenes. Use a refrain to transition between the scenes and include a poignant inference, somewhere in the work.

HER IMAGE

All I have is her smile
in an old Polaroid.

She took the picture herself,
and her face is far to the right and low.
But in the background you can see
some of my things,
evidence
she once stood here
against the backdrop
of my little radio,
nightstand, unpaid bills,
water-stained sheetrock,
and I think that's one of my paintings there
in the corner.

She walks with God now,
but I keep her picture on the radio,
and sometimes
I turn it on,
hold the Polaroid,
and dance with her in my mind.

The Writer

When I was younger, I "went around" with a girl who I'll call Eve. After a party with a hot tub and too much alcohol, the sun had come up, and she was leaving. Back then, I slept with the covers pulled tightly over my head. It kept the bugs off and the cold out. She said bye, and I didn't even poke my head out. I just slid my arm out and waved.

Years passed, and I moved into the trailer park where her parents and sister also lived. Eve had been married for a few years by then and had a kindergarten-aged son.

I met her sister while walking one evening on the road; we clicked. Within a few days, I'd gone to her house and met her mother and father. We began walking with one another around the park, talking and enjoying the out-of-doors. She was great.

One night, we planned to meet for spaghetti at my place, but she never came. I called, but she wouldn't answer. Later, I found out that Eve's husband strangled and stabbed her to death, and then came a few trailers up from mine and strangled her 61-year-old mother, too—all in front of her little son, who the father afterwards abandoned in a hotel lobby. Eve was also eight months pregnant.

I never saw or heard from Eve's sister again.

Much later, after I'd moved to Corpus, I learned Eve's murderer was the 382nd person executed in the state of Texas since the reinstatement of the death penalty.

Over the years, I've thought about her, diffused snapshots of memory, clouded with the shame of my behavior.

The Polaroid is imaginary. When I heard about the execution, I lived in the apartment I used for the picture's backdrop. The photo has become my private way to visit her a moment, and to maybe say I'm sorry.

The Craft

In as much as the piece centers on a Polaroid, I use visual imagery as the prominent mechanism. "Selfies" are common these days, but back when photos were developed only on film, if people took pictures of themselves, they were usually being silly.

I imagined her holding the camera out and taking an off-center photo of herself. To my mind, it's more flawed and human than a perfectly centered, well-snapped picture.

The picture's setting provides a secondary characterization of the speaker that reveals his economic status with unpaid bills and water-stained sheetrock.

The speaker says, "She walks with God now." This euphemism[13] is intentionally indefinite. This is so that the reader may easily make the inference, and perhaps recall a person they knew who has passed away.

The Invitation

Write using a real or imagined picture, to trigger memories from distant eras of your life.

Maybe you're like me and have done something to atone for, or feel sorry for some way you have behaved. Alternatively, maybe you have someone you miss, and for a moment, you can interact with him or her again in verse.

---

[13] euphemism is a mild or pleasant word or phrase that is used instead of one that is unpleasant or offensive.

THE BOY

Here he came.
Click, click, click, click . . .

A little too dressed up to be
thirteen and riding his bicycle around the
apartment complex.
Loafers on, shirt tucked in,
dress belt, pimples cosmetically concealed,
hair perfect.

Click, click, click, click . . .

Cool. Standing on the pedals,
snaking across the parking lot
in lazy half circles.

He stopped at the corner of my building where
the little girl below me lived,
then leaned his bike neatly against the bush,
checked his belt and the crisp tuck of his shirt.
He ran a little plastic comb through this
copper hair, then disappeared around the corner.

Knock, knock, knock, knock
. . .
Knock, knock
. . . . . .
Slumped, he re-emerged,
slowly reclaiming his bicycle,
sat heavily in the seat
and rode away.

Click, click, click, click . . .

Better luck next time, kid.

WATERBALL CAROUSEL

I had given her a carousel.
To wind it
was to play

"You are my sunshine, my only sunshine,"

beautiful music,
melody to sing my feelings.
A crystal globe
fit around it,
and if shook,
glitter floated up,
gold,
then settled down.

It wasn't much,
but I had thought
it something pretty.
She knew that,
and in a rage

"You make me happy when skies are gray."

broke it
against the linoleum
in the kitchen
of our trailer.
Water flew out
in a rush of
sparkles

". . . my on-ly su-nsh-ine."

and broken glass.

Quiet . . .
I listened
to the few bars of music
that played,
wound
by the shock.

The Writer

The Boy

Standing on my balcony one day, overlooking Oso Bay in Corpus Christi, I saw this little boy with copper hair clicking up on his bicycle. He may have had beads on his spokes that rattled as the wheels turned, but I heard him from a good way off. He did his best not to race over, being casual, snaking his bicycle, cool.

Below me lived a pretty little redheaded girl, 13 or so, whom he had come to visit. Unfortunately, for all his Sunday best and effort, she was not home. I've struck out like that a few times myself, so I felt for him.

The poets of Corpus Christi roasted me when I moved to Dallas. They dressed like me and read poetry written in my style or about me. It was great! They were some of the best friends of my life.

My late friend Dennis Flynn asked for this piece to roast me with. He read a kindness in it and thought it represented an unusual example of my work. His interest in this piece changed its meaning for me.

Consider this:

Writing is generally a solitary craft, but going public with your work doesn't have to be. In your area, there are poetry communities. You can often find these by looking for open mics in coffee houses and bars.

These places offer excellent opportunities to share what you're writing, and get to know others you will hear whose work you admire. Here you can form a peer group to offer you honest criticism (if it's a good one). They can have a positive impact on the quality of your writing.

Often an open mic will have a featured poet, meaning they have invited someone to read for fifteen minutes or so, to break the ice, affirm the theme, or to showcase. Once you have established yourself and proved you can hold a crowd, these opportunities will open up for you as well, but you've got to get out and participate first!

Waterball Carousel

Being now rather sophisticated and debonair, I've learned that, in the parlance of our time, these are called waterglobes or water globes not waterballs. And if they're full of snow and a winter scene, they are called snowglobes, not snowballs, and they certainly aren't meant to be thrown like a snowball.

My first ex-fiancée had a bit of a temper and a great pitching arm. One day while we argued in our trailer, and I don't know what I did (probably nothing; I'm always innocent), but she threw a water globe with a carousel inside it at me, which I dodged. Thank God for being fleet of foot! That thing had quite a heft. It shattered and played the remnants of a song, which rang most inappropriately for the moment.

The Craft

The Boy

The prominent mechanism of the piece is onomatopoeia "click click click" and "knock knock knock." followed by an ellipsis to indicate time passed. As with any punchline piece, the setup is key. Here the majority of the poem is dedicated to the buildup of his arrival to the little girl's front door, with the way he moves indicating his emotions. At first he is "cool, snaking across the parking lot," later he is "slumped" and defeated. This builds tension for the character's anti-climax and the speaker's dry, summary remark.

Onomatopoeia— words that sound like what they describe, such as drip, splash, howl, and whine.

Waterball Carousel

While this piece does not use onomatopoeia directly, it implies sound through the interspersing of a well-known song that interrupts the narration and stands ironically against the speaker's situation.

The Invitation

Write being conscious of how you illustrate sounds in your work. After the initial draft, reread and consider what your piece has given the reader to hear.

Try a poem in which you experiment with sound words, or well-known passages of music, that either stand in ironic contrast to, or in agreement with, the message of the work.

THE SUNNY SIDE

She was drinking orange juice and ice cubes
raving about her husband's shocking temper
and the static she had with her in-laws,

the cleaners lost her slacks,
and the movers lost her underwear,
an angry, dark rant,
and my only response, the only one I could get in
was "I see. I see."

She was on the curb, and I in the street.
The sun shown behind her
like a great electric light
glowing through the thin yellow linen
of her sundress.

"I see. I see," I said.
Finally, she concluded, after she'd bared her soul saying,
"…but I always try to see things on the bright side. Don't you?"

and I said, "Indeed, I do!"

The Writer

Throughout the '90s, the sundress was big fashion. I always thought these looked sexy. My first ex-fiancée, being a true Georgia peach, loved wearing them, and I loved to see her in them. Linen at sunset might as well be cellophane.

The Craft

The sun-color motif works with the idiom "sunny side of life"— a pun for my male character's optimism as he listens to the female character complain, standing with her back to the sun (the sunny side).

> Pun—a word play that relies on the different possible meanings of a word.

In my memory, static cling and sundresses are synonymous. So, I added the slang "static" (meaning problems) as a pun in the first stanza. I then juxtapose her "dark rant" with the light shining behind her.

At the time of the writing, a friend of mine had told me the movers lost her underwear, which I thought was completely bizarre and funny, so I added that to the stanza as well, ending with the line "I see. I see," where the male character ostensibly affirms his understanding, but means it literally.

In life, we sometimes find ourselves accidently (hopefully accidently!) in the direct line-of-sight for something not intended for us see (in this case, it is straight through the female character's dress). To capture that in a poem, I had one character standing on a curb to elevate her and assume the distance necessary for the other character's eyeful.

> Idiom—an expression whose meaning cannot be predicted from the words that make it. This can be a saying that is dialectical, regional, or characteristic of a particular era or person.

To reinforce the situation, I punned with the idiom "bared her soul" which to her meant shared everything, but to the male character meant she, well, shared everything! So again, I contrast what was figuratively intended (by using an idiom) to how it was literally received.

The poem closes with the final irony of the two characters seeming to agree over what she had argued, while the reader knows that they essentially had two completely different conversations, which simultaneously transpired throughout the piece.

The Invitation

Write a poem in which the characters experience a disconnect between what one character figuratively intends (by use of an idiom, or misuse of an idiom, as the case may be) and another character literally interprets. Keep it subtle or be outlandish, but if you think hard enough, you can probably recall a situation not so different from the one I wrote about.

For example, back when I tended bar, a waiter came over and said he'd embarrassed himself. A customer had said she felt so full she needed to grow a second stomach. And he said, "That's okay. I had to grow a third leg!" In his mind, he meant a wooden leg to store the food in, but of course, that little explanation never made it out of his mouth, and he sounded like a creep.

Once you have your setting and problem, decide how your character reacts to it. Do you have them feel supremely embarrassed or shamefully interested (like my character)?

THE FLOWERS

She sends letters from England,
thought of me while musing on
the sunflowers of Van Gogh.
It has been nearly two years since we've talked.
She slapped my face after Bob Dylan
in Houston, and I gave her my back.
She couldn't take it that she loved me,
a desperate one-sided love.
She continues to attempt contact, but I'm silent.
Our friendship faded with the echo
of violence.

It's not that she frightened or hurt me;
it's that she
crossed into a theater men and women
should not enter.

Van Gogh painted sunflowers in pain,
wilted, naked of their roots, dying on the table,
with thick impasto and busy strokes.
She,
like him,
spent time in a mental institution,
but it had no view like Saint-Remy,
and no one brought paints or called.
I do not expect her ear
as a token of love,
but I know,

that like Vincent,
her sunflowers are in pain, too.

124

The Writer

A brilliant woman from Kentucky befriended me in my twenties. Wealthy and educated, she became one of my best writer friends.

W.B. Yeats and Van Gogh fascinated us. In our writing, we experimented with density, creating a menagerie of symbols, making simple things complicated and occult. I picked up painting around that time. Color blind, I tried textures, swirls and impasto like Van Gogh—but badly, no doubt.

It ended up that she loved me more than I did her. When I called it off, she couldn't easily let go.

She sent dozens of beautiful post cards bought at the Van Gogh museum. She called during late hours and sent letters. But, since I caused the pain, I couldn't console her. Our friendship busted, and she lost her mind for a while.

Old paintings, Sunflowers, took on new meaning.

The Craft

Art as motif is the saturating concept here, and it is set up immediately. The next thing established is the conflict, then the distance of setting. The speaker is in Texas. The female character is in England. This connotes emotional distance between them as well. The dominant shift in the work moves from the explanation of the situation to the symbolic connection to the painting, which seems quasi-ekphrastic in the way that it illustrates the emotional, personal connection to the speaker's situation through the visual imagery describing the painting.

> Ekphrastic poetry is poetry written about or in response to another work of art.

The stanza structure is eleven, four, eleven, two. The eleven line stanzas address connection: connection to one another, connection to the art. The four-line stanza is near the center of the poem and addresses the consequence. The two-line stanza is half the four-line stanza, representing the fading echo, the wilting end.

The Invitation

Write a poem that connects your personal experiences with art. Consider what stands out about the work you've chosen, and then define the painting through the metaphors you make. For example, in my poem, the cut sunflowers dying on the table held the pain that symbolized the situation with my friend. That painting summed up my feelings at that time. From there, I integrated it into the story it represented.

SHELTER

Today I heard a young and pretty woman, shading beneath a sun
umbrella
complain she's led a sheltered life
She wanted to see the world
"Merry-go-rounds to porch swings," she said
"What happens to us along the way?"

I wish I had known her well enough to say
"There is nothing wrong with shelter
The world can be a maelstrom of painful, ugly things

With age comes focus
Focus isn't as fun or reckless as we'd like
but it's efficient, healthy

Porch swings have that easy glide with only
a soft push of the legs
Merry-go-rounds are faster but too much work
They leave you dizzy
out of focus

When the sun and sky are this bright
when humming birds are dancing
and the breeze is right
do not complain that the world has not been harsh enough to you

How many days of rain before another one like this?
Who will complain about shelter then?"

But I said nothing
shrugged
and we watched her children play
from the shade of her sugar-white umbrella

The Writer

At one time, I went out with a girl who said, "Chris, I usually date doctors and dentists—big business types. All their money is great, but sometimes I just like hanging out with a guy like you." I think that was supposed to be a compliment. Somehow. Evidently, she thought slumming with me gave her authenticity--not unlike those writers, or recently music performers, who flat-out invent hardship so they have some kind of flaccid credibility.

Don't feel sorry if your life wasn't hard. Keep living, and the rough spots will find you. Until then, just be yourself. Pretending anything else makes you look like a shmuck.

This poem is an amalgamation of several remarks and conversations from over the years—and how I've bitten my tongue.

The Craft

The first three lines establish that words were spoken beyond the boundaries of the poem. The two speakers shelter beneath a parasol, with the female speaker lamenting her sheltered life, establishing shelter as a motif. The children are not sheltered, lending a subtle, but contrasting characterization that perhaps they are out and experiencing life.

The merry-go-round, classic playground equipment, symbolically contrasts the porch swing, which (stereotypically) older people use. The implication is that these represent the beginning and end of life, respectively.

This sets up the situation for the main speaker to offer his insight, which comprises the bulk of the poem.

Symbolically, the color white symbolizes purity, and sugar is sweet. So I imply, through symbolism and connotation, the woman's purity from being sheltered is sugar sweet.

The Invitation

Write a poem about a moment in which you've had to bite your tongue. Introduce the setting and characters, reveal the advice, and then turn away having said nothing.

If you can't think of a time you've stifled your unwanted advice, try it; you've kept it "too real." In one shot, you'll both earn an idea for a poem, and the people around will appreciate your company for a change!

BENEATH THE BEACON OF MARS

She was a heart-shaped box
of chocolate mysteries
I was a broken nose
running in the light
of the low harvest moon
wrecked on a folly stone boulder
near a robin's vacant nest
where stoplights and stop signs smolder
      ignored by Corvettes and fire engines
      racing quick as red
towards the flames of passion or madness…

Fainting,
falling,
I dreamed she spun out of a rosebud
throwing sparks
singing perfume
      a modern madrigal
in the sweetest fandango
lilting harmonies
that made me feel she could make the crooked straight
while a ladybug on an apple sang along
sipping a first vintage sauvignon
with lips and nail polish shining
in the night's bloody November candle

Walking, I skulked,
sulking busted,
silent,
half-cast in shadows blushing—
unable or too wounded
to risk rejection's crimson trudge
or judgment's razor edge

too bent to breathe
her song.

The Writer

Lawrence Ferlinghetti's use of metaphor in *A Coney Island of the Mind* struck me in a way that I had never seen. It seemed he took a concrete item, made it an abstract idea, then into a new relative concrete item and back to an abstract idea. I've since gone back through the collection looking for the piece he did that with but could never find the line again. This could be a great example of misprision; either way, he taught me something about a metaphor.

> Misprision—misreading or misunderstanding a text.

To offer an example of what I thought I saw him do, the movement might go like this:

> A raven,
> a worried glance,
> a spot of ink,
> shadows,
> eyes darkened with shame,
> discarded letters never read.

There's a thread of diffuse relationship, but it is full of gaps. In those gaps, readers can co-create meaning, adding layers to your poem.

The Craft

Playing with the associative aspect of the metaphor, I made a game of listing all things red. Then I began creating metaphors with them, matching the things and the expectations of those things (the connotations they carry) in unusual ways such as "quick as red," and "singing perfume." I developed a Frankenstein/Princess contrast between my characters, and began to work in items from my list. I even played with etymology, using Madrigal, a spiritual song which was usually sung by multiple voices (in this case, my speaker might like to sing along, but cannot), but the word "Madrigal" shares a common root with the word "Matrix," from the Latin *mātrīcālis*, which means "from the womb," which I would also consider red.

Fandango is both a type of red and a dance. So, again, not everything in your writing has to be obvious or even reasonably ascertainable so long as these tiny nuggets remain small details and not critical to the overall sense of the work. Some things we can hide for just the extraordinary reader and ourselves.

The Invitation

Write choosing a color that has multiple associations (both abstract and concrete). This will serve as the motif of your piece. Find a contrast and begin working associations together to create a cohesive piece of writing.

Sift through the diffuse threads of metaphor; you may surprise yourself with what you come up with. Do a little research into words, and enjoy your thesaurus for a poem like this.

CALLIOPE BLUE

She weeps jazz,
something slow from a sobbing trumpet
where notes carry little caskets of echoes,
lost "love you's" that never made it
past the twisting nether of her doubts.

She sits on her favorite chair breathing history—
woulda's and coulda's
in the reverb of obsession.

A metal trashcan rolls by like brushes on cymbals
singing out a shush
like tumbling,
splashing shad fish
across the electric silver of her pride
that's so mud-caked and sunbaked hard
she's nearly forgotten how pristine it is when shined

She's got icepick heels and a dancing dress dusty in the closest
that have made men's hearts skip to cut time
in some ragtime blitz of goofed smiles,
but she never wears them.
It's not her neckline; it's her lip that's lower than a doghouse bass.

The soft murmuring trumpet of her suffering fills the room.
If it were a little more muted
and her hearing sharper,
she might perceive the distant dirge
of a lonely man tapping on the blacks and whites,
dreaming of a soft, jazz rag doll
to jam with.

The Writer

In 2013, I read at the Kerouac Fest in Houston. It was an amazing event with brilliantly read excerpts of Kerouac's work, facts about his life, new Beat poetry, live jazz and free beer. Although I could not drink all the free beer myself, you must know I absolutely did my best.

When I wrote the poetry for the festival, I didn't know if the jazz band would back me up or perform at another time. Therefore, I wrote imagining room to pause and let the music bleed around the words. As it turned out, I read it straight.

The Craft

In mythology, Calliope is one of the nine muses—a daughter of Zeus and Mnemosyne. She is the muse of epic poetry, but all the muses are associated with music and dance in some way. In this poem, I imagined her lonely and blue.

Diction builds atmosphere in writing. The collective connotation of words builds an emotional motif. So, here I open with words like *weep*, *slow*, and *sobbing*. I use a variety of alliteration to create and carry sounds that lend themselves to the internal music of the poem—the jazz of imagination.

I use a diffuse style of metaphor. Here is my process: I've always thought brushes on a cymbal sound like a rolling trashcan lid; trashcan lids are silver; fish are silver and boil in a froth of many tumbling fish; silver is a proud color, a precious metal; a person's pride might shine silver.

The Invitation

Write using metaphors that extend and change properties. Consider a kind of music that you like. Set up a contrast between two individuals, and build a motif using images that are archetypical to the genre. Be diffuse. Let your subconscious surprise you.

THE STUPID THINGS WE DO TO DEGRADE AND KEEP OURSELVES ENTERTAINED

She said, "I can tell you're unattracted. It's your body-language."
"My body is multilingual," I said. "Maybe you misread it."

But when I turned away, the side of myself nearest her went dead pale.
"See! See there," she shouted. "You're doing it again."

I shrugged. "No problem," I said. "You're in luck. I don't have anything to do tonight."

"What's that got to do with it?"

I didn't reply and ordered another whisky… a double this time.

The Writer

I've had many bad dates. There's always that miserable moment when the wheels fall off, everybody's trapped without a drop of chemistry, and we sit struggling through small talk shackled by our own politeness, amazed that we have once again chosen so badly.

She was an internet date. Her pictures were remnants of the "good ole days," maybe from a previous life. Maybe she found those pictures in a purse she snatched. I had no patience for deception. Even still, I'd driven a long way to meet her, so it was too soon after sitting down to run away. Since I had already dressed in my darkest, cleanest t-shirt with a fresh haircut, I figured *hakuna matata*. We met in a bar, after all.

The Craft

The main elements here are dialogue and contrast.

The tag in dialogue denotes who is speaking, such as "he said," and "she said." Keep it simple and stay with "said." Do not substitute adverbs into the dialogue tag. Don't say, "she mocked," "he mused," "she grouched," "he stormed." If anyone is mocking, musing, grouching or storming the dialogue itself should reflect it. Build the situation well, and you don't have say "she replied tersely." The sharp rebuke will be timed and stated as a sharp rebuke. You may even go one further, and take a tip from Cormac McCarthy, and skip the dialogue tag all together, except when it's necessary to keep the speakers straight.

The Invitation

Write a poem in dialogue. Use an exchange between speakers. This could be aloud, or you could write one character as speaking, while the other character remains mute but thinking the replies. You could have two speakers in an exchange that a third interrupts. You might imagine two people only thinking as they pass but never actually speaking at all.

Keep it short and centered on the poetic moment.

CALCIUM

Leaning against a tree listening to tiny gray birds
sing from wires and phone poles in the easy Saturday sunshine,
I think, "Man, if I had my own little kid,
we could hang out on a day like this!"

Then a tiny girl runs by wearing a pink shirt,
the sweep of her jeans a pulsing whisper as she carries past singing,
"Step on a crack, break your mother's back…"
skipping joints in the wide sidewalk

until she comes to a long jagged crack.
She pauses. She doesn't see me watching.
Her cute face twists down, evil. She begins laughing like a hyena
hunched over something doomed,

then leaps and smashes both feet right across the crack.

A branch snaps and falls from high up in an oak tree.
A squirrel chatters about something urgent and unlucky.
The girl runs on,
and I decide that perhaps I don't yet have a strong enough spine.

The Writer

Leaning out an open doorway, I watched while children ran in the afternoon. A little girl skipped by, pigtails bouncing, singing, "Step on a crack, break your mother's back," and she leapt and stomped on a big crack in the sidewalk. I found it so surprising that it stayed on my mind until I wrote about it.

The Craft

This is a basic misdirection. I knew the surprise of the ending (because it surprised me), so I set up a pleasant day with which to juxtapose the subject's actions. The speaker's dialogue at the end also contrasts his feelings from the start. This is one of the shifts in the poem.

When the tiny girl is introduced, she is intended to seem cute, small and (at least on the exterior) innocent. The main shift in the piece occurs between the second and third stanza where she, melodramatically, reveals her inner self, which is quite the opposite of the speaker's perception. The drama of the revelation affects even the setting. The tree cracks; the squirrels chatter; the speaker changes his mind.

The Invitation

Write considering what is perceived versus what is real. Reflect on the face we show the world.

- What do we keep for just ourselves?
- What do we truly desire and seem to desire?
- What do we think about others?
- How do we appear to think of them?

Give this mask to a character (speaker or subject). Use contrasts and juxtapositions to achieve the transformational effects—characters in poetry can evolve and change their minds.

TOMCATS

She loves this cat
this street fighter
who only comes in for a meal
then screams by the door until it's opened,

this creature that prefers the hollowed log
of the ash tree to the comforts of indoor confinement
who never comes when called, nor leaves if he has chosen to stay
who can be incredibly grouchy and then just as sweet.

She pours the dust of catnip
into the corrugation of a cardboard
scratching pad, which he destroys
in the most shameless ecstasy.

Then she brings me a beer
and I ask her why she loves
this trollish little cat so much
and she says, "He reminds me of you."

The Writer

Half-chewed pecans pelted our cars, the deck, the house, even our heads. The squirrels were destroying my nuts! I went from thinking they looked cute and fuzzy to seeing them as my grandfather did—fluffy-tailed tree rats! So my lady and I went down to the pound to find the meanest, toughest, orneriest cat in the whole place, the cat no one would want because all he knew how to do was kill small fuzzy things. And we found him.

At first we thought he might be an indoor/outdoor cat, but he howled his howls so quickly and loud, one after the next, they tripped over one another, piling in our ears, cacophonic and ceaseless. He never got tired yowling for infinity or until we let him out.

We named him Virgil, after the author of the *Aeneid* about Aeneas who was good at fighting and killing. Virgil the cat has also authored many deaths and wars. He did battle with every cat in Houston, killing all the squirrels, mice, mockingbirds, lizards and bugs he could creep up on or run down outright. More brutal than any shark of the seas, he always had some helpless prey.

The Craft

In fiction, the secondary character's only job in the world is to tell us more about the primary character. This poem is a punchline piece. The whole poem builds the character of the cat then shifts, revealing a metaphorical connection with the narrator.

The cat is actually a secondary character. This is also an example of indirect characterization, where one character (the narrator) builds through another's reactions, thoughts and comments (in this case, his female friend).

Indirect Characterization—character information revealed through his thoughts, words, and actions, or through how other characters respond to, or think about, him.

The Invitation

Write a conversation between two characters: one character describes and the other listens. Then, create an ironic revelation, a shift, which metaphorically connects the description with the listener. This can be for comic or serious effect.

The Pilgrim Within

The alarm didn't sound.
Nothing bit or ran across my body,
but my eyes opened.
I couldn't see the clock,
too much cluttered the dresser.
It was still black out,
but I was awake,
more awake than I could ever remember being.

The sheets were kicked to the yellow-green linoleum
of my tiny trailer floor,
and I was upside down.
I showered, dressed, and stepped onto the porch.
Looking out across
the rectangular lots of tin homes,
I could still see some of the fading stars and airplanes
flashing off into the distance.
The trashcans were full,
so I dragged them to the curb.
I usually miss the garbage men,
but I'd catch them today.

I reached down and took up a scrap 2X2 to fend off dogs
and strolled to the end
of the block to a cemetery.
I'd never walked there before.
My father and I would walk by old graves reading
tombstone dates and inscriptions
when I was a young boy,
and we did our best to walk between them.
It was an old cemetery
with graves dating back to the late 1800's
and the most beautiful drooping cedar trees I'd ever seen.
For a while, I walked and read,
admired men of wars and sadly noticed children
who had not lived long.

I found a cracked concrete bench in a dark cluster of cedars.
Someone had propped it
so half was flat and I sat there,
tapping my stick on the other half.

142

The evil lay next to the saints.
All kinds from plot to plot, and so many stories.
A garden planted with the dead.
But it didn't feel like death around me. Felt like peace.
Plato said, "Only the dead have seen the end of war."
I'm ready for the end of war:
the war inside,
loneliness,
self-abuse.
Peace beneath cedar trees is very satisfying.

If I could create my life moment to moment,
become the vision
and soak the wonder of the present,
I could glow from the inside.
Laughter would no longer be a sedative,
but wild dances from a happy soul.
Sparrows sang in the branches above me,
and when I looked to see
there was the sun,
boiling and exploding at the center of our solar system.
I felt clean among the dead.

When I stood, something ran into the underbrush and disappeared.
The devil maybe
or an angel who had seen me through?
I took my walking staff and left the sweet smell of the trees,
following stones, reading.
I dusted grass and leaves from one
and inscribed was "God Bless Him. Our Amazing Grace"
I don't know why,
but I began to sing.

". . . to save a wretch like me. . . ."

I was a wretch
with barely a roof and food to keep me hungry.
Someday, I told myself. Someday, life will be more
than leftovers.
I dropped my head, so no one could see,
and I wept,
walking back past the junk lots
back into the trailer park,
singing softly to myself
as I went.

The Writer

Living just off a graveyard in a poor trailer park with murderers, drugs, thieves and wife beaters wears on a person's self-esteem. You start wondering, if in reality you don't fit right in.

Under that kind of stress, life was a hum of work, depression, and dissipation. Until at last, I found days of clarity, times when a feeling of intense motivation and house cleaning overtook me-- times when my spirits filled with the idea that I was better than where I worked and lived. This is when I set new goals.

But, I felt lost much of the time. In my heart I was a fighter, yet I had days so oppressive that they might get the best of anybody. But what do you surrender to? The graveyard was just down the street.

When I needed answers, I read. I read like mad, and I went out to meet and hear others who wrote. I listened to other poets in the city, and I learned from them. I read head-to-head with them. They became my friends.

I knew that still, essentially, I was alone, but not completely so. And that felt great.

I ran across John Gardner's *The Art of Fiction*, in a used bookstore. When I read his advice saying that great writers read widely and write prolifically, I had hope. I was already doing that.

I agree with the writers who argue that writing isn't something you do only when you're inspired, when you feel like it, or when you have time. Whoever became a champion, or a master, by being a flake?

Writing nightly will record your cyclical life. If you're living a broken record, you'll notice it. You'll notice it, notice, notice, notice, notice it. Once you do, you are smart enough to adjust. Some of my favorite pieces grew out of compulsory writing. I saw I was writing the same old thing and changed it up. If it was sad, I gave it hope; if it was lonely, I made someone show up.

We can fall into habits of sick thinking. Nightly writing records our habits and excuses. By repeatedly chronicling the same poem, the same behaviors, the same causes of our failures, we tire of our own stupidity. No one wants to say, "I've written one poem over and over for my whole life, and it was a bad one."

Nightly writing is good for creativity and breaking bad habits.

The Craft

Allegory is a form of extended metaphor. In one regard, the poem's speaker takes a walk through his neighborhood; in another, metaphorical sense, he takes a pilgrimage for a little soul searching.

My character begins his day upside down—his position indicating this day will be opposite, or at least much different, to prior days. He drags out the trash, foreshadowing a cleansing of sorts. But first, he walks among the dead.

Historically, those who dealt with and handled the dead were considered unclean and not allowed to re-enter the city until completing religious cleansing rituals. So when my character says, "I felt clean among the dead," that alludes to how religiously "filthy" he felt, or at least how filthy that he felt that he was.

In the "wilderness," that dangerous area beyond the known world, ogres and dangers[14] lurk. Here, stray and vicious dogs haunt the character's wilderness. Literally, they do not appear in the narrative; however, their rumored presence adds to the atmosphere of the character's day-to-day environment.

His "pilgrimage" is to a cemetery, a clear symbol of mortality and appropriate for reflecting on his life. There he recalls his father (revealing a little of his past, values and circumstance) and contemplates his own situation. The bench he finds is broken. Contrasting the idiom "no rest for the wicked," he sits on it and taps his staff against it, perhaps distancing himself from the wicked. However, the character himself is unsure. When something stirs in the underbrush, he wonders if it is a devil or an angel who has seen him through.

This piece contains a series of allusions that follow in rapid succession in parts. Observe:

---

[14]See *Hero With a Thousand Faces* by Joseph Campbell, or *A Writer's Journey* by Christopher Vogler for more on the hero's journey monomyth motif.

The line, "Laughter would no longer be a sedative but wild dances from a happy soul," is a blend. Part of it comes from my recollections of a girl who once told me that when I laughed it seemed that in that moment all the stress and worry lifted away, and I looked happy. However, the stress and worry soon returned. The other part, "wild dances from a happy soul" alludes to W.B. Yeats' line in "Sailing to Byzantium":

> An aged man is but a paltry thing,
> A tattered coat upon a stick, unless
> Soul clap its hands and sing, and louder sing
> For every tatter in its mortal dress,
> Nor is there singing school but studying
> Monuments of its own magnificence;
> Therefore I have sailed the seas and come
> To the holy city of Byzantium.

I borrow Yeats' scarecrow metaphor for the body/soul relationship. Also, Yeats wrote a book called *A Vision*, and I allude to that when I say, "become the vision and soak the wonder of the present." (Admittedly, my *A Vision* reference is so puny even Yeats himself wouldn't recognize it. However, to my mind it exists… if but barely.)

"Soaking the wonder of the present" alludes to the Eastern concept of the never-ending now. If we take full advantage of the present, we will have had a good past and will ensure a great future.

I tried to let the allusions flow one atop the next. Whether anyone understood those allusions, or even found them, was no reason for me not to add them. They were not key to the overall meaning and were subtle enough that the majority who missed them would still have no trouble understanding the work. They only offer another layer of interest—for both a reader and myself.

The sparrow was a symbol of Aphrodite that meant true love. At Troy when a snake ate nine sparrows it was prophesy that the war would last nine years. In some folklore (mostly European), if a sparrow flies into a house it's a symbol of impending death. In Indonesia, a sparrow flying into the home means good luck. According to the ancient Egyptians, sparrows carried souls to heaven, yet in their hieroglyphs, the depiction of the sparrow meant "bad" or "small."

In the ancient Christian tradition, the very poor gave sparrows as offerings to represent God's concern even for the very small.

The sun, to alchemists, was a cosmic power, and the symbol of the mind. Alchemy relates to Yeats, as well— spiritual alchemy with the transmutation not changing lead into gold, but from body to spirit.

"Amazing Grace" is my all-time favorite song because of the history of it, the lyrics themselves, the way it moves me. I put it in the poem, at the end, but I didn't want to quote too much of it because that had a banality I wanted to avoid. Plus, when I read it live, I'm not about to stand on stage and sing a few bars. Some like doing that. I'm not one. The song is too good to trivialize and wreck like that.

In truth, that tombstone I described doesn't exist. I made it up as an approach to work the song in.

The piece ends with my character walking back into the park. Not every journey ends happily or in a terribly different place than it began. The elixir (lesson) this character returns with imparts that sometimes, even though it's hollow, we must return to where we came from—until the day we don't. But that takes time.

The Invitation

Write a journey piece. The journey doesn't have to be epic. In my example here, it's a walk to the cemetery and back.

As Joseph Campbell said, "You are the hero of your own Story." He also said, "As you proceed through life, following your own path, birds will shit on you. Don't bother to brush it off. Getting a comedic view of your situation gives you spiritual distance. Having a sense of humor saves you."

You live a life worth writing about, and you will return with many different elixirs from many different journeys. So pick one and begin.

Consider this:

What kind of traveler are you, and how does that relate to the nature of your journey?

Is it a spiritual quest, a quest that forces you to face something you've ignored?

What is the elixir that you return with? Is it a lesson, a self-realization?

Pepper in pertinent lines of philosophy you've picked up in life, but do it like tasteful jewelry. The right type of stone in the right setting looks beautiful. Too much, too fast, too big or too obvious looks tacky. If you aren't careful, you'll come off like a try-hard. So, keep it subtle.

Also, consider your favorite writers. Is there an allusion to their work you can make? What symbols can you add?

Create or revise a journey piece into an allegory by adding a motif of symbols, relative philosophical quotes and literary allusions. Bring your character back with some form of elixir (message or lesson), or at least the piteous realization that your character has yet to find it.

I WALK

I walk,
no silver heel
tap prance,
clickety-stomp, Fred Astaire,
River Dance
step.
Just steady
metronome
deep echoing
through gray stormy birth days, sunny death days, hellos and see-ya-
laters.

I live
without roots,
an abstract specter
distant from mindful friends
who worried
when I left without turning off the light
and never came back.

I hear
enlightenment is beneath the feet
and to find it one must
step after step
overcome, progress,
learn, and survive.

I've watched
men wither in sickness,
seen charcoal smiles mock pretty things,
been the prodigal son for too long.
This path is trampled to cracking earth.

So I set bootheels in a new direction,
to travel lands I've never seen,
use these fists to shake men's hands,
not have to watch my back,
and to wrestle with love for the first time.
I walk
but

I could use some company.

The Writer

This piece pretty much sums up my 20s. I was destitute, volatile, depressed. But I always had books and writing. In *The Book of the Five Rings* Miyamoto Musashi[15] describes fighting as walking, moving. With my being an avid martial artist back then, I took that to heart, and knew if I kept going through the worst of it, then the best of it— life—would finally find its equilibrium.

Colonel Sanders of Kentucky Fried Chicken (whom I quote because his chicken is so delicious) said it best: "People will rust out quicker than they'll ever wear out, and I'll be darned if I'll ever rust out."

The worst thing we can ever do to ourselves is stop.

The Craft

Each stanza begins with an anaphoric, short sentence (I walk, I live, I hear, I've watched, I set). Then, each stanza elaborates—a vignette, or snapshot pertaining to some aspect of the speaker. These elaborations define the character and lend impact to the speaker's invitation for the reader to join him.

Anaphora is the repetition of a word or phrase at the beginning of successive verses, clauses or sentences.

The Invitation

Write a piece of short vignettes that all work together to make a singular point. Start each stanza with a reaction of the senses, a new place or mood. You could illustrate an insider who wants to be an outsider or an outsider longing to be an insider. Take the persona through various moods or reactions in the work. You might even have completely different characters that see a single thing but draw various conclusions. Be sure to keep the reader's take-away message clear and singular.

Consider how your poems move. Examine the kinds of shifts you use.

---

[15] Miyamoto Mushashi (c. 1584 –1645) is considered by many to be the greatest swordsman of all Japan.

BENCHED

Shuffling over to see my bookie,
on the poor West Side,
I'd often see an insane vagrant
wearing a Texas Ranger's batting helmet,
shouting at no particular thing
from a very old, gray bus bench.

Some days he'd sit on his feet
and wave a string of large plastic pearls
like Buddhist *mala* beads, mouthing *dharanis* and *sutras*
            only he knew.

Once in the spring
I saw him sitting Indian-style in a patch of weeds
by the baseball diamonds
caressing a seedpod of Johnson Grass.
I had my window down as I rolled by
and heard him exclaiming, "Brother grass!
            Brother grass!"

And I remember last Tuesday,
when it rained like hell,
            he took shelter
beneath the dirty red big top
of a Christian Ministries Revival tent,
and was sitting on a white and blue
            "Take it to Jesus!" sign
though empty chairs were available.

This Sunday, as I slept in,
because I never go to church, I thought about him.
With more religion than anyone I know,
he's either got his bases covered
or loaded,

with Buddhist Monk on first,
Medicine Man on second
and Christian Preacher on third.

It would seem he's rich in spirit,
but indigent, busted flat and nothing left to bet with,
he's striking out with both God and country.
I'd lay wager that Confusion is pitching
and no runners will ever make it home.

The Writer

Windblown litter, broken furniture, broken people—all common sights near my street in Corpus Christi. And knowing that a great portion of the homeless population is mentally ill, I wrote this piece to make a comment about those I would often see, as there were—unfortunately—so many around.

The Craft

Like "I Walk," this is a chain of vignettes, in which the speaker describes a series of religious identities portrayed by the subject. The last stanza brings them all together to end in a sort of punchline—his overarching observation.

The subtle red-white-and-blue motif is meant to juxtapose this character against sacred colors of our country for the obvious shame that here in our wonderful nation the mentally ill homeless are so common.

The subject also contrasts with the speaker, who never goes to church. He explores many religions but finds himself caught in the same conundrum with both country and church. He has no answer for either, and thus he will never make it home.

The Invitation

Write a piece describing a thing in three stages of time: cattle—in winter, fall, summer; a bud—closed, in bloom, wilted; a couple—shy, in love, lonely. Allow the setting to interact with the subject. Create a motif to tie the stages together.

Working for Intrinsic Value

Tina lives alone.
Her house is impeccably clean.
She has a cat named Family
that is mostly white with spots
of red, yellow, black and brown.

She works a job that pays her poorly
but it has intrinsic value.
She barely makes her bills,
and work is mostly
what she talks about.

She tells everyone she is beautiful and smart.
It seems she pleads with them to believe it.
She keeps plants and does wonders with them.
She makes phone calls to tell people
when her cactus is in bloom.

There was a time
she thought sex would bring her love.
After many tries
with many men, she
changed her mind.

Today after running errands for her mother
who she resents in many ways
she put on tight jeans, contacts,
and took a great deal of time
with her makeup,

then went to the store for the ingredients
for her famous white enchiladas.
She caught looks, gave looks.

For a moment felt good,
but no conversation progressed past hello.

She checked out and returned
to her one-bedroom apartment and cat.
Hating to cook for just herself,
she went through
a paper of friends numbers.

Everyone was busy.

She put the ingredients in her refrigerator and cabinets,
opened another new bottle of red wine
and ate fists full of cheddar goldfish.
and when she was drunk enough to no longer care
she cried
late into the night
holding a small mirror,
watching every tear
wash her mascara
in black streaks.

Before the room began to turn
she set a razor and pills
next to her bed
hoping she would pass out
before Courage came to use them.

Clicking off the lamp
she lay back on her beautiful bed
with all its pillows
and let herself pass out.

She couldn't do it tonight… but tomorrow was a new day.

SHE WAITS DREAMING

You wait dreaming like a fossil
passing a comb through the acreage of your hair
like a tractor busting earth
with Hope singing in a crooked cavern of your heart
to hieroglyphs, petroglyphs, painted oceans and painted ships
daydreaming one day an albatross
like a good Christian soul will bring you north again
and with dental picks and brushes more delicate
than those in your vanity
clean away all the wasted moments, regrets,
all your insecurities and
wire you back together
to exalt the treasure of your heart—

Your fine suburban home has become
your own lost Abydos[16]
and you dream like something trapped in amber
for someone to look into your dark eyes
and say, "I see wonderful things."

---

[16] Abydos is one of the oldest cities of ancient Egypt and the site of a great necropolis where early pharos were entombed.

The Writer

Working for Intrinsic Value

I had a friend who, in spite of her extreme beauty and fun personality, suffered from loneliness and depression. She would tell me about her evenings of sitting in the candlelight, after cooking a meal no one showed for, reading tarot cards for herself. She kept a strong outer image for most people, but I knew her. Some nights when she couldn't keep the facade any longer, she pulled down the Goldfish snacks and a bottle of wine then fell to pieces on her living room floor.

She would call me, swearing this was it, the night she would kill herself. Then I would come over and finish her wine, so she could sober up and get herself back together. Luckily, she had great taste in wine!

The last time I saw her she was getting married in a coffeehouse courtyard, dressed like a pixy, skipping through the bushes trailing pastel scarves.

She Waits Dreaming

This piece isn't about a particular person. I wrote it while feeling depressed that so many fascinating, valuable people sit waiting to be discovered, alone. And how they often have a great deal of personal philosophy built around their seclusion.

The Craft

Working for Intrinsic Value

Tina's cat is the colors of humankind. She could be anyone.

<u>**Consider this:**</u>

Instead of saying, "Tina is lonely," (a vague picture), I emphasize her loneliness by giving her traits that round her out as a character:

> She keeps a clean house, has a cat, wants to cook for groups of friends who aren't available, shops alone, and finds self-esteem in her low-paying job. She compliments

herself, since no one else does. She has made many bad decisions regarding love.

Beware of simply *telling* in your work. Scan your early drafts to highlight these merely didactic moments and re-evaluate them as candidates for revision. As a writer, you may hold an image in your mind that these telling lines do not relate at all. Instead, *show* your descriptions by appealing to the senses, so that these images transfer from your mind to the reader's.

The scene builds towards a moment of pathetic desperation in which she calls everyone, but no one answers. Then I show her giving up, putting everything away and feeling small and lonely. Watching her tears fall, she becomes a spectator of her own sorrow. Oftentimes, we are excellent at recriminating against ourselves when depressed. She fantasizes about suicide but can't do it, which is also common.

Using a bit of verbal irony, I change the context of the idiom "But tomorrow's a new day!" to emphasize that for some the hope isn't for improvement, it's for courage to bring the end.

She Waits Dreaming

I use two main allusions for this piece: Egyptian iconography and Samuel Taylor Coleridge's poem "Rhyme of the Ancient Mariner."

The crux of the piece centers on the idea that we all want to feel valued. However, too often we find ourselves alone with nothing but a mirror for company. I imagined a lady's makeup desk with her seated at it, beautiful and wanting to feel admired, but no one is there.

I refer to a famous verse from "Rhyme of the Ancient Mariner" that reads:

> Day after day, day after day,
> we stuck nor breath, nor motion;
> As idle as a painted ship
> upon a painted ocean."

I also reference ancient drawings hidden for millennia in caves and tombs and all but forgotten.

These references illustrate her as fossilized, forgotten and frozen in her own solitary habits. She waits undiscovered but hopeful like the immense wealth hidden in a forgotten tomb, covered by time.

The Invitation

Consider this:

Though writers may seem to write from someone else's point of view, we may actually use another person's story as an opportunity to confess or vent some weaknesses within ourselves that we're otherwise unable to write.

Write a moment (real or imagined) from another's point of view. Treat your characters honestly, considering them as human beings as you create the work. Hide your flaws and insecurities in theirs.

REMEMBER WHEN THE CHURCH BELL BROKE

Remember when the church bell broke?
It hung like a hymn in an angel's throat.
That winter's dawn played off icicles like sitar notes
while the engine hummed its deep, bass drone.

With no radio to pass the miles,
we had conversations you never heard.
The cold air had made you tired.
We had no heater and you reclined half-bobbing in sleep,
curled under a U-Haul blanket

while hawks watched from the tallest, thinnest branch
of ice-mummy trees, reflecting on the geometry of their latest trophy
catch,
and the cattle watched,
huddled under lone pasture oaks
thinking jack shit while we sped by dreaming of distant beauty
and answers to all mysteries, understanding we would never know
them,
hoping only to know them better.

When it came to love, you thought I was like a cow
thinking jack shit because I said so little, but each mile
I thought about how we went together
like gall bladders and folk cures, sunshine and sunburns,
PETA and fake fur, fishing and earthworms,
the '70s and home perms, the Old West and butter churns,
disco and heel turns, ashes and urns.

You always worried I would leave,
but you got hips like a dashboard dolly,
can hold your liquor and make me happy.

You say I'm like a spider, in my Zen alone
in an attic somewhere, rarely if ever seen by another's eyes,
but I get hypnotized
by the settling house, the settling dust,
accumulating rust, and the tracks of the mouse.

You help me remember not to live in a snarl,
and just because trouble finds me,
it doesn't mean I always bring it on myself.
But I can still throw a knife or hatchet
with hair-splitting accuracy
just in case I need the help.

Because the gargoyles in my growl often fail
and life's golden shine goes winter tarnish.

The mile markers call, and it's time to go,
but I'll no more ride alone...

I'm bringing you with me.

The Writer

I wanted a journey piece that focuses on a couple who loves one another but has a terrible time expressing it.

As a kid, I remember taking long drives with my grandparents from Oklahoma to Iowa to visit my dad and uncle. They never played the radio. Walkmans, iPods and cellular phones didn't exist. The only entertainment I had was a BB maze game. So in the bumpy backseat, I would try to maneuver a small ball bearing through a plastic maze by tilting it this way and that.

Mostly, we all looked out the window in silence. But, my grandfather did love pointing out big hawks on thin branches and fence posts. To this day, when I pass them, especially in Oklahoma, I point them out, too.

This piece captures the dynamic between my third ex-fiancée and me, though I don't recall having her specifically in mind at the time of the writing. She loved to travel. I could rust up at the house. When we finally did take our romantic trip to Colorado, I nearly killed her in a wreck.

The Craft

Wondering what kind of music that light would make shining across icicles, I decided the coolest would be from a sitar. Using tiny wind chimes or the like seemed too easy and not very spiritual sounding.

I use indirect characterization to round out the speaker. Though the reader never hears the girlfriend speak, we get to hear her thoughts through the speaker himself. With her asleep, he can finally reveal his feelings.

In my list detailing how they go together, I purposely paired unusual items to make the list sound fresh and illustrate the speaker as clumsy with love. I made all of his examples rhyme for humorous affect and ended on "ashes and urns" because, though it's an awkward topic for him, he is sincere—clearly a "till death do us part" allusion.

Consider how flat the last line would read if I had written, "I'll not ride alone anymore." It also gives away the ending and negates the need for the final line. Instead, by using the unusual word order of "But I'll no more ride alone," it continues to communicate the subject's awkwardness for the speaker and maintains the impact of the last line.

Even when I write a piece for performance, like this one, I make sure it also works well on the page. Always consider how your piece will look apart from the performance.

Consider this:

If I drop a stanza or two this piece will time out right at three minutes. In today's performance community, a three-minute poem immediately qualifies as a candidate for slam. So, if I slammed this piece, I would choose it for at an outdoor venue or for a more conservative reading.

When choosing work for performance, consider the venue. Readings at the local library or the Barnes & Noble tend to be more conservative due to the presence of children. Adults like to get rowdy but not in front of the kids. Respect that. Outdoor venues also tend to be more conservative. Coffeehouses can go either way. If you're reading in a bar, bring on the rough stuff.

I've had luck with this piece in all of the above. So a piece can be child-friendly and still maintain its edge.

For longer pieces like this one, a single shift usually isn't enough. The writer must offer readers, and audience members, constant surprise.

Those who slam with one-dimensional pieces, fluffed for the three-minute limit, make it hard for an audience to enjoy them. We get bored. All the shouting and real tears in the world won't sell a trite, diluted three-minute rant that cannot stand apart from its performance.

Slam—poetry performance of original material where contestants are judged by pre-selected audience members and rated on a 1-10 scale, decimal points accepted, usually for a cash prize.

However, if the piece evolves with fresh imagery, multiple shifts and honesty, the audience will more easily remain engaged. An engaged audience is a happy audience—which means points on the judges' score cards.

The Invitation

Write a longer piece letting some of your stanzas indicate shifts. Structure it so that the piece unpacks, moves, and feels fresh. Try to engage the audience with constant surprise.

Avoid a prose telling. Examine each movement of your work for the poetic devises that you used. Quantify them if you have to. This will improve the impact and art of what you're relating.

Using metaphor and analogy to communicate more effectively is a mark of intelligence. Their usage will also give your work the powerful touch of originality.

Whiskey In A Ghost Town

A gambler or gun for hire it was all the same to him,
a different man, another notch or dealer deal again.
The posses that have chased him would have liked to see him hang,
though few are alive, for most have died when the sound of his six
gun rang.
The horse he rode, a Comanche paint, he'd stolen long ago
from an Indian in a knife fight down south in Mexico.

His bottle glinting and three-quarter drained of a dead man's rotgut
wine,
and boots that boast his father's spurs of silver and design
made this man with haunting eyes and hat of faded black
glow eerie in the ghost town with the sunset at his back.

Crunching cemetery sand crust, he crossed to crush the men
who with rattlesnake mercy hogtied and murdered all that ever
mattered to him.
One last drink, drunk to her memory, before he ordered them out to
the street,
then threw his bottle through the bank window to get them to their
feet.
Seconds later, several faded from the shadows into sight
expecting talk, but what they got was flashing iron sights!

He cut one from the balcony, one from the saddle,
one through the chaps who dropped and soaked the gravel,
one near the hotel steps, one through the neck
who gurgled half his insides out before he hit the deck.
He never stopped moving; he was here and then was there.
His aim was ever perfect while their bullets sprayed the air.

He killed one near the water trough who splashed in with a lurch.
But, the bullet from that shot struck a statue in the church.
Before one misfire, two misfires opened him to attack.
One outlaw with no ammo licked a bullwhip 'cross his back.
He spun and like a hammer threw his one misfired gun
and squeezed the other's trigger while his target staggered stunned.

The worst of those he'd ridden to see
seized upon the moment to charge back from retreat.
Seconds fractured like stained glass. Everything went cold,
but the burning through his back had his reflex slightly slowed.
Their next volley caught him; two bullets had found home.
Clothes darkened at the wounds where his hot blood flowed
With anger he aimed and continued to unload.

The last two stumbled forward and tumbled stone dead.
The last of his rounds emptied each of their heads.
He stood for a while alone in the sun
He'd earned more notches for the grip of each...
His six gun slipped from his pale, clammy hand
And he dropped to his knees in the hot summer sands.
Wagon wheels and tumbleweeds was all there was to see
the lone desperado who lay dead on Whiskey Street.

The Writer

This poem took me 18 years to finish. I began it in 1992 when I was 18 and a private in the army at Fort Sill, Oklahoma. At the time, I idolized Henry Wadsworth Longfellow. His cadence, rhyme, and ability to take me somewhere with a story. Observe these lines from his poem "The Village Blacksmith."

> Under a spreading chestnut tree
> The village smithy stands;
> The smith, a mighty man is he,
> With large and sinewy hands;
> And the muscles of his brawny arms
> Are strong as iron bands.

Blues legend B.B. King said, "If you see someone doing something you like, borrow a little." I interpreted his quote to mean that eventually imitation gives way to internalization, and I could create pieces that are more authentic in time to come. In these early story poems, I simply wanted to do it like Longfellow— tell a vivid story and rhyme (though I did not slavishly follow his rhyme pattern).

I worked these poems so repeatedly in my mind that I would memorize them. Other soldiers on guard duty with me would often ask to hear them to pass the time. During one cold November night in basic training, while guarding a pile of coal that no one wanted to steal, my friend Waycaster asked (while we tried to take our minds off how cold we were) "Hey, Wise, you got any poems about a cowboy?" I said, "No, but I will."

Unfortunately, the Army assigned us different bases after basic training, and Curt never heard the poem I wrote for him. After 18 years of revisions, this poem was published in 2012 in *Cowboys and Indians Magazine* online, which has a readership of over 800,000. This was my biggest publication to date.

It is my homage to the spaghetti western.

The Craft

Rhyme as a law in poetry is out of style, but since this is a classic subject, I think the rhyme works. If we do use rhyme, we want our rhymes to sound fresh. Unfortunately, in English, most of our words end in consonants, so it's not as good a language to rhyme with as, say, Spanish, where most of the words end in vowels. However, we have many tricks other than hard rhymes to find music in English. We can use near rhymes such as assonance and consonance. The traditional hard rhyming sound is often called a "true rhyme."

Assonance—vowel sounds within a word.

Consonance—consonant sounds within a word.

Another way we create music in our language is through alliteration.

In the lines "Crunching cemetery sand crust, he crossed to crush the men…" I stacked the alliteration there to try to create the impression of crunching sand. Alliteration, used like this, can create onomatopoeia.

Here, using inference as a tool for characterization, I gave the character his father's silver spurs and the remnants of a dead man's bottle of wine. These insinuate a small amount of depth to the character. Story people come from somewhere and have a life history that started before the story begins. Be aware of this, and offer this depth to your characters. Sometimes the questions we (as writers) generate are more interesting than the ones we answer; they offer additional layers of discovery for readers.

In this piece, I created my shift at the point the bullet strikes the statue in the church (shooting Jesus is bad luck). As Jesus was a sacrifice, my character is also. In fiction, it is interesting to make likeable characters and kill them off. Both classic and modern authors do this with powerful effect.

The Invitation

Tell a story in rhyme. Be vivid, and let it play out like a movie. Try to not just use end rhymes, but also play with the internal sounds of the piece as well by using alliteration, assonance and consonance. You don't have to kill your character, but remember this: many consider Emily Bronte the greatest of the Bronte sisters because she was ruthless to her characters, as was Shakespeare to his.

Our characters are not our children. They are constructs we use to achieve visceral effects in our readers. Don't be afraid to write them a life of hardship if somewhere there's a payoff for the reader. Charles Dickens did it and made a pretty good name for himself! Also, consider your shifts. How does your poem evolve?

TAPESTRY OF HEADS

A tapestry of severed heads
bound with hairs of golden thread
carols for rhythm
while I sleep

Twisted and bruised with bloat and rot
noses withered, eyes in knots, they keep the beat
for nightmares that plague
while I writhe in slumber

Naked heels on crushed stained glass
dance it down to blood and sand
while lizards—the sun's most holy followers—
bob their heads and sing of Armageddon
In each of their pockets burn rubies:
reminders of God's red fire.

But I am a beggar with no precious stones
left alone
to wander the wastelands, a pauper
with only echoes in my outturned pockets...
The echoes of hands and fists striking
stainless blades shining
distant voices crying
and music from a carousel

Evil things prey upon me
in my deep repose
choking me
until I finally
explode from dream, knotted in sheets
gasping for a voice to scream
into the tumult of the loveless night:

"Why does it take so much sorrow
to purchase one moment of happiness?"

The Writer

Once in 1987, while I was playing at the trestle near some junked out cars, a scrap dealer grabbed me and dragged me through a junkyard. He accused my brother and me of setting his cars on fire and busting his windows. We wouldn't have done that. We were just too young to have the proper idea of what "Private Property" meant. Though I struggled my best, he had me by the collar, punching me in the neck until I let up or got the wind to struggle again. This was especially painful because only a few months before, I'd gotten my head nearly scissored off in a small elevator with no door. He locked me in an office.

Luckily, my little brother ran for home to tell my grandparents who phoned the police.

When the police showed up, he changed his tune, of course. Suddenly, he became mighty concerned we'd drown in the "thin water" of his ponds, which were flooded coal pits—whatever thin water was. I remember him saying, "Oh, that's Old Man Wise's boy? Well, I bought chickens from him!" Like he was a real family friend. I chewed a hole in my lip to stop myself from crying in front of him. It would have humiliated me worse than I already was.

In 1989, my friend and I walked by Lake Dallas near our homes. A group of men partying at the lake mistook us for someone else and beat us with tree chains and stomped us until one of the men pulled a .38 and threatened to shoot us. We ran.

They filled a utility van and a Mustang when they gave chase. The Mustang hit me in the back of the legs, but we had already run for my friend's porch. Bloody and lumped, we barely made it inside before they caught us again. His dad went out with a shotgun and a handgun, and they fled.

In 1998, three guys tried to force their way into my apartment, and I fought them off with a sawed-off shovel handle until my neighbor called the police, and they fled.

In 2002, teaching school in South Dallas, a guy in a Chevy Astro shot at me while I was breaking up a 15-person gang fight out back of the temporary buildings. The bullet missed me by about six feet—a terrible shot, really. But, the intensity of the situation, mixed with my pushing them all to the right while the car rolled left must have thrown him off. He fired one round from about 30 feet out, and I could smell the report.

Growing up, I often had trouble like that. Maybe the stress and worry of it all caused the nightmares.

I do not perform this piece.

The Craft

I pulled the word tumult from Yeats' "Irish Airman Foresees His Death":

> Drove to this tumult in the clouds;
> I balanced all, brought all to mind,
> The years to come seemed waste of breath,
> A waste of breath the years behind
> In balance with this life, this death.

Though his poem had a completely different message than mine, there was a relative feeling I recalled due to how he used the word.

The faces of the hanged knitted in tapestry, groaning, twitching with the incredible speed of a suffering, dying thing was like a skipping record. It hurt to see and hear them hurt.

This writing is a conglomeration of nightmares: a carousel of the dead, lacerated feet, the heads, all resolving with the question asking why happiness felt so rare.

As writers, we must even put a nightmare to work. I kept a little diary of dreams. When I went back, some dreams made sense, some made no sense at all. Some had a twist of interest, some I tore out and threw away.

Concern for the mechanism of rhyme (in all its textures: soft and hard) carries a give-and-take where the effect is concerned. I could have skipped the rhyme and focused on the grotesque for more horror. But, I chose to keep it syllabically relative and in rhyme for the spell-like chant, which went better with the whole of *Thirsty Earth*, the collection I worked on at the time.

I use a montage of nightmares—pictures of unease—and my borrowed word from Yeats' poem for the emotion it lends.

Here too, I included symbols: the desert lizard standing for the austere Christian who exists with nothing between him and the sun/son; the ruby is God's self-portrait, a crystalline representation of God who appears as fire.

These symbols, in conjunction with the speaker remarking that he has only echoes in his outturned pockets, intimate that his connection to God is impoverished, as he has only memories of the past. With no God, the door opens for the evils that haunt him.

The Invitation

Write about the nightmares you have. Keep notes or a diary of interesting dreams. You may craft these into interesting pieces. Also, just writing about nightmares and worry brings them into a physical, manipulative state that for some reason makes them easier to tolerate.

Our dreams are, in essence, a puppet show that the brain creates to make sense of and work out our emotions. They are our own private myths. Some, in fact, are so supremely personal they do not adequately transfer to the language center and lose their meaning when retold.

The dreams we can share do not differ much in structure from fictions we might create. In as much as these stories are essentially founded in emotion, we can see how so many stories throughout the world, throughout cultures and time, might often have so many uncanny similarities.

I Never Spoke to Atlas

At zero in the frankincense
I move stoic past fallen pillars
that pock white and gray
the glade where the Titans died.

Then fades sun and shine,
sound of surf, and smell of brine.
I'm overtaken, spirited away
by an all-consuming fog.

There is woeful singing in the air.
I know the words from another dream
though unwilling, I too begin to sing
feeling this other's despair.

Suddenly, I find myself in the abyss
stepping on stars to make my way.

I see Atlas, the source of the singing,
kneeling and leaning
the world low on his back stretching high.

Before I ask, he reads my mind
and says he weeps for what he must do.
The world, he goes on to say,
has of late fallen to decay
the way it always does
when it slips low upon his back.

Soon again he must juggle it up
for a better grip
and seat upon his shoulders.

The Earth will shake
when its great plates slip
and tear her rocky hide,
the molten tides will flow and rip
and scorch the earth alive.
This is why he weeps, he says.
This is why he weeps.

I formulate another question
but he knows the answer still before I speak.
Civilizations will fall away, he says.
Many will be lost to time,
but some will be found again one day.
And just enough of the ancient's ways
will remain
to be baffled by their wit.

Atlas lowers his head
beginning again
his dirge.

When I decided to sit and wait,
sing with the god and avoid this fate,
I was taken again by the fog
and returned to the smells of frankincense

where I half-dreaming heard
sirens racing by
outside in the night
and my neighbors loud
next door.

The Well at Auvers[17]

Never safe in a dream
while the soul vaults in quest
delving into worlds
beyond the realm
of consciousness

I've been in the church at Auvers
and seen in its basement bones
especially by the well
There from the darkness, I heard the drone
of the troglodyte's lonesome baritone
and grew ill from a carrion smell

So terrible my tremble
I tensed and nearly woke
but relaxed at just the moment
before the vision broke

I sunk into the well
past much slimy brick
the walls clenched about me
till I reeled near faint and sick

The cavern at the bottom
was a den of puddled ponds
where a heatless shabby lantern
flickered poor illumination
on infant bones like cobblestones
and his draconian mutation

Shattered idols strewn the floor
weakly reconstructing
then crumbling, crashing down once more

---

[17] Auvers-sur-Oise was the place where Vincent van Gogh spent the last 70 days of his life. He painted approximately 70 paintings in that time, including The Church at Auvers (L'église d'Auvers-sur-Oise, vue du chevet).

believers numbered few and poor
too weak to keep them standing

Near a corner crystal pool
the lizard man knelt weeping
His ruby eyes scorched rippled water
across the darkness gleaming
while he droned a prayer
tripping weakly from his lips
murmuring through echoes
in cadence with the drips
falling like full tears from high
since the last of the last apostles died

       "Here though shadows scarcely move
       they're pregnant with their secrets too

       Sorrowful Mothers their fresh-born rained
       to this stony floor
       female babes who'd never sing
       knotted with their birthing chords

       This well has hushed the suicide
       falling from the top
       and from the stealthy murderers
       caught their silent crop.
       Clumsy drunks and hopeless brides
       gazing from the rim
       have met the ancient, crumbled idols
       who have waved them in

       I have known them all
       tender soul to busted bone
       the last to lick their worried ears
       with my whispered baritone."

I stumbled back half-drugged
to clear my foggy mind
His change of tone brought welling fear
the fire left his ruby eyes

He dropped his thin veneer

A hive of roaches stormed the sides
spinning through a smoke of flies
that choked up with the sulfur
stinging through my squinted eyes

He lurched
wild for my throat,
his face a foul contort
an umbilical that tied his navel
to the cavern floor
sung out like fired bow
and stopped him dreadful short

In sheets, twisted, wide awake
tethered to my bed
the comfort of the crunching mattress
quickly cleared my head

vanished was the vastness
of the black and murky cave
the grotto of the troglodyte
and its many secret graves

My Van Gogh framed in plastic
cracked and fell from the nail
the traveler, reversed in graphics
walked the other trail

How like the lizard his disguise
How lit with fire his diamond eyes

I had met the evil one
in gestation as he spawns
Already he has taken lives
spanning ages all
I have seen the first to come
when Armageddon calls

178

The Writer

I Never Spoke to Atlas

The wonders of ancient civilizations have always fascinated me: the moving of a 100-ton block without heavy machinery, the nearly perfect calculation of the earth's circumference, and megalithic constructions resting in perfect alignment with the stars. Yet in some cases, the people who accomplished these miraculous feats seem to have disappeared abruptly, along with the science they developed.

I imagined a meditation in which I meet the Titan Atlas and discover an explanation for why earthquakes happen.

During the writing of this poem, I studied a movement of writers (W.B Yeats, T.S. Eliot, Ezra Pound, D.H. Lawrence, etc.)[18] who felt that they lived as part of a natural aristocracy defined not by social class but by education and creativity. The coinage of their morals and artistic creation elevated them from the ranks of the proles[19] to those of the bourgeoisie with more life-flame than a dull clerk who eats tinned meat. Mass man[20] was to them a thousand-headed worm, the great unwashed, or mackerel.[21]

The term "natural aristocracy" came from intellectual exchanges between Thomas Jefferson and John Adams. In a letter written in 1813, Jefferson wrote to Adams, "For I agree

---

[18] See *The Intellectuals and the Masses: Pride and Prejudice Among the Literary Intelligentsia*, 1880-1939 by John Carey.

[19] "Proles" is a word coined by George Orwell in Nineteen Eighty-Four that refers to the working class of Oceania, i.e., the proletariat.

[20] "Mass man" was coined by José Ortega y Gasset in *La rebelión de las masas* (*The Revolt of the Masses*). It was published as a series of articles in *El Sol* in 1929 and as a book in 1930 with the authorized English translation published in 1932. Ortega sees the mass man not as a member of a particular social class but as part of a large number of people who try to suppress or destroy anything that is different, individualist or highly creative.

[21] Mackerel is a food fish, which does not leap above the surface and gathers in dense schools of many thousands. I believe the term was applied in the same manner one would call another a sheep.

with you that there is a natural aristocracy among men. The grounds of this are virtue and talents."[22]

This was a natural exploration for me. There's no doubt, I had tired of tinned meat, well aware of my own dullness and wanted to align myself with these thinkers.

These years later, I feel differently, actually preferring the working class point of view and writing with the more simply stated line, but that was an important tangent that left an indelible mark. Creating and using my own symbols in a personalized mythology made me more aware of symbols in the writings of others; counting syllables and writing in rhyme improved my attunement to meter and sound.

So I offer the point that as writers we will have phases of interests and periods of testing our voices to sound like this-or-that, him-or-her. Take from these digressions what you need, but once you tire of them, move on to your next exploration. If we're honest, our growth is more amoebic—stretching us into what feeds our curiosities—than it is linear. Each phase we traverse brings us closer to mastery. And mastery is attainable!

The Well at Auvers

Anyone who has visited Auvers should immediately see through me. I have not! Not only do I not know if there is a well in the basement, I don't know if there even is a basement.

Actually, I bought my print of Van Gogh's "The Church at Auvers" off a street vendor, and it was so bootleg, the lady walked up the wrong side of the path. It was printed backwards! That's what made me think to add the detail of the lady moving up the other path, but I used that image archetypally to connote that things had changed and to assist the surrealistic quality.

This piece is in *Thirsty Earth*, the same collection that contains "I Never Spoke to Atlas." But here, instead of using Greek myth, I used the Christian mythos and imagined an encounter with the antichrist in the womb.

At the time of the writing, I read *The Secret Doctrine* by Madame Blavatsky and writings associated with *The Golden Dawn*,

---

[22]See *The Founders' Constitution*. Volume 1, Chapter 15, Document 61.

as well as experimenting with meditations through *The Irish Celtic Magical Traditions* by Steve Blamires. They helped to satisfy my interest in the study of the occult, inner-alchemy, the supernatural—magic.

I focused on that painting during these meditations, and this poem represented, in its earliest draft, one of them. However, this was not spiritual in any way.

To me, meditation invited logic to connect the diffuse ramblings of a relaxed mind in order to create something meaningful and unexpected from the subconscious. Revision, no doubt, worked away inconsistencies.

The Craft

I Never Spoke to Atlas

Any time I've carried something heavy for long enough that my muscles failed, I've had to pause and jostle it up for a better grip or drop it. I gave Atlas this same problem except, as the planet slides lower, so does the morality of civilization. Then Atlas has to juggle the weight up, "rebooting" parts of the world and causing natural disasters. This piece imagines why civilizations rise and disappear.

Atlas is greater than mortal, so I wrote him as telepathic, reading my thoughts and knowing what I would ask before I did. Then once I had answers beyond the knowledge of man, I tried to avoid our inevitable doom, but I could not, as we are all cast together beneath the net of heaven.

The Well at Auvers

This piece recalls *The Church at Auvers* by Vincent van Gogh. Not quite ekphrastic, I offer it as another example of myth making in poetry and connecting art to myth.

The troglodyte, a man-lizard (in this work lizards symbolize the austere Christian), would seem to be Christ returned, but he is instead a man-serpent. Satan appeared as a serpent. Therefore, who (or what) my character perceived as a troglodyte, in actuality, is Christ's warped mirror.

I also used rubies as symbols of God's presence (God appears as fire) and diamonds as symbols of God's absence, as diamonds steal the light they refract and are colloquially referred to as ice. The fire alludes to Dante's myth that imagined Satan existing in the lowest, most frozen deeps of Hell in a place most removed from God's Light (and presumably his warmth or love).

The Invitation

Write incorporating symbols into your writing. If they are nonce, make sure to define them clearly in the piece. This is only a form of metaphor.

Nonce symbols are symbols created by the writer that are unique to the occasion of the poem.

Once you have created several symbols, take on an idea (political, social, religious, philosophical), and blend them with some form of mythology that complements your point or adds a desirable effect.

See Appendix A for a brief discussion about considerations to make while reading myths.

New God Paradise Fisher

In the brine drunk for line
the Sirens sing to me.
Boon voices echo thrice
pledging allocated paradise.
In rapture, they take me in a dream.

I the king, they my brides
palace throne 'neath the tides.
Strong, wroth my trident stirs.
Ships like rain, monuments—sepulchers.

No life measure, treasure
collections of pleasure
Alea reach, beg embrace
title me god, paradise I taste.

Faith twisted, voice says it's wrong
to enjoy the pagan song.
I steer to the east, the Sirens quiet at my right.

The Sun lights; they fade from sight.
Sober now the tide has changed.
At last, I see the other whose acquaintance is strange.

Genesis new, changing time.
The One knows; the Sun will shine.
Perfection fished from the brine.

The Writer

You can take your symbols too far, becoming so allusive no audience will care enough to tease them out to find your meaning, which may not sound as profound as you might have hoped.

I've included this piece to demonstrate how it appears when you've massively overthought a poem and used a thesaurus for words you didn't even know five minutes before you dug them out and dropped them in.

I'll never forget recording poetry on cassette while drinking whiskey in my friend's garage. Matt Leal threw a party and drifted over my way while staggering on a pair of roller skates, honking a clarinet. I showed him this piece. He flopped down in a lawn chair and said, "Chris, anyone can dig up big words to try to sound profound. But true genius reveals what's profound in a common way for everyone to understand." Then he tottered up and skated off with a shovel in his hand to smash a piñata he'd draped over a limb with an extension cord.

His comment forever changed the way I write.

The Craft

I attempted to write about a person living during the changing mythos who had decided to turn from the worship of Poseidon to Christ. At some point in history, that decision faced people, and I thought it sounded interesting.

I wanted to establish the brine as the abyss; with "drunk for line" meaning my character had no direction. Three sirens attempted to exploit the speaker's confusion promising immortality, wealth, a kingdom beneath the sea—he could have a power like Poseidon himself. However, in actuality, they would do what sirens do best and kill him.

The shift comes at the fourth stanza when his faith twists. The sun rises in the east; Jesus is supposed to appear from the east, so the character steers in that direction. To the right of east lays south. South metaphorically aligns with Hell, obviously.

With this, he finds light, a clear mind and paradise.

I used words like "Alae," which unless you speak Latin or had a copy of my enormous thesaurus, you wouldn't know means "wings." And I referred to God as "The One" as the Norse referred to "The One Too Mighty to Name."[23]

My valiant effort or a waste of time, either way, I think it's a flop. Yet, it represents one of the best lessons in writing I've ever had and worthy, if only for that, to share.

The Invitation

Write without overdoing it. Remember, too much sugar cloys. Too much salt poisons. Don't let the message be lost to the mechanism. And, don't be so clever that you actually look foolish.

---

[23] See *Myths of the Norsemen* by H. A. Guerber

Form

I Wrote Your Name in the Sand With my Finger

I wrote your name in sand with my finger,
but a quick crab chased me away before
I could time the surf to write anymore.
A wave crashed, effacing all the letters.

That was the last day we were together.
Our romantic evening along the shore…
I can still see the bikini you wore—
racing through the surf for the gull feather.

Now, flown seven-thousand miles away
I'm in armor with a rifle in hand,
wondering why time is stuck marching in place,

thinking of you as often as I can,
wanting to talk, but unsure what to say,
except I'm still writing your name in sand.

Iophon[24] Speaks

Thank you for the writing lessons, Father.
My plays have gotten so moral and tragic
only Euripides[25] can best me.
Admittedly, I took some of your themes,

but I did them with a more modern feel.
I shuffled *Iliou Persis* [26] and ran it.
I tried no plot, no rhyme, nameless players—
I set trends. My friends are the It crowd.

You, my father, are getting so old.
Oedipus at Colonus [27] will not last…
enough with gods, love, and fools humbled!

And, all that money you horde should be spent.
I'll take it now and say you've lost your mind.
Why do you cry, old man? I am the future.

---

[24] Iophon, fl. 428 B.C.—405 B.C., was a Greek tragic poet and son of Sophocles.
[25] Euripides, c. 480 B.C.—406 B.C., was a Greek tragedian whose works include *Medea, The Bacchae, Hippolytus, Alcestis* and *The Trojan Women* among fourteen surviving others.
[26] *Iliou Persis* translates as *The Sacking of Troy.*
[27] *Oedipus at Colonus* was the last of Sophocles' Theban plays, written shortly before his death, which describes the tragic end of Oedipus' life.

THE CONFETTI OF DECAY: SONNET I

I look round, sad, bothered by where we are.
Nose pinched, casting votes, hearing we are free.
The world over, people want to come here
to escape tyranny, poverty, war
so their families can live without fear,
prosper, have health care, a piece of The Dream.

Yet, for its points, we've no castle in air.
God is gone on all except our dollar.
Debt has crushed us down to just a prayer
while taxes have us wondering what's fair,
and the poor fight wars the rich wouldn't dare;
I am poor, and what have I but honor
and what was granted us by our founders?
I do my part… while feeling no one cares.

THERE'S SOMETHING IN THE WAY SHE SCREAMS

There's something in the way she screams
Where the birds fly away and the cockroaches hide
And her white teeth glisten with her mouth open wide
Hissing caustic-sunshine-acid fog that lingers through my dreams

On the black velvet frame of night, lit with rhinestones and LEDs
A sulfur wind blows grim and dim, boiling as it glides
While she heaves raging, flushed and glassy-eyed
Quaking on the quiver of the hangers-on leaves

November breaks like dark lake ice
Nothing feels sealed well enough
The witch of winter bites
Through gloves, parkas and earmuffs
And the reaper waits on the slicks to strike
Between the ice and the tire and the oak tree and the bluff.

CONTEMPORARY GENIUS

Aristotle wrote of contemporary genius
References of delight we should match as we might
Polygnotus,[28] Pauson,[29] the artist Dionysus[30]
His superlative ideas for us to abide.
Men whose creations echo faintly from the eon
Stuck resonate chords in the organs of those before
Careful craft innovating catharsis and tension
All hourglass drowned, deeper than Ozymandias.[31]
Nothing but their names remain, proof in ancient essay
We are left to wonder at the bliss to which we're blind
For even the essay itself only partly remains
The rest hard-locked behind the unfathomable hasp of time.
> While currently, we have here, in our time, in our town, near our homes,
> great poets, artists, playwrights who are restless, unheard, ignored, alone.

---

[28] Polygnotus, c.460 B.C.–447 B.C., was a Greek painter who was born in Thasos but became a citizen of Athens where he painted his most famous works depicting superior people. None of his works survive.

[29] Pauson was a Greek painter of whom little is known. He is believed to have lived in an earlier time than did Aristotle. He painted his most famous works depicting inferior people. None of his works survive.

[30] Dionysus was a Greek painter of whom little is known. His painted his most famous works depicting his subjects just as they were, neither more beautiful (as depicted by Polygnotus) or less beautiful (as depicted by Pauson).

[31] Ozymandias, c. 1303 B.C.—1213 B.C., alternately called Ramses II. However, this allusion refers to the sonnet written by Percy Bysshe Shelley (1792—1822) who began writing the poem after a massive head and torso fragment was removed from Ramses II mortuary temple in 1816.

THE ELEPHANT MAN CROWN: SONNET I

Half-meals in half-light, a turnip in broth
sloshed down with a curse on the plank table
so fiercely it stirs a solar-white moth
to flutter up to the vaulted gable
I tremble, trapped, in perfect misery
beneath her sneer while Father brings the lash…
both revolted by my deformities
Love is scarce as turnips, but beatings last
I used to flail my legs to duck the switch
as they mocked me for not earning my part
but then Father somehow crippled my hip—
while beating the devil out, broke my heart
    "Jesus, in Heaven, makes the crooked straight,"
    I sobbed,
     wishing I'd the gable-moth's place

The Writer

I Wrote Your Name in the Sand with My Finger

My time in the military was unremarkable compared to the service of many, but I'm very proud of it. I served as a 13B (cannon crewman). It was my job to load, emplace and fire the M109 A3 Self-propelled Howitzer. Though I nearly deployed on several occasions, the country never sent me to war, but we trained constantly. We spent many nights in the Mojave Desert at the Army's National Training Center (NTC) in full chemical warfare gear, in temperatures that reached upwards of 120 degrees.

Being young and in love, the time away from my lady seemed like forever. As a writer, I bent this experience towards the perspective of one who missed a loved one while deployed. I hoped that this poem might offer people in the speaker's situation a way to share their feelings.

Iophon Speaks

When Sophocles was 90, his son Iophon took him to court in an effort to swindle his fortune, claiming the old man had gone senile. Sophocles produced a selection from his play *Oedipus at Colonus*, read it in the courtroom, and the judges dismissed the case. Wondering what Iophon could have been thinking, I researched to learn more about him, and wrote to explore his mindset—in my opinion.

The Confetti of Decay

I wanted to write about how I felt in the world. I didn't intend to specifically criticize or lay blame. I simply wanted to discuss my personal observations, as a nobody, a person lost in—and among—the masses.

There's Something in the Way She Screams

At the time of the writing, a terrible auto accident killed a family after icy roads caused their car to slide out of control and strike an oak tree.

Recalling a line from Gordon Lightfoot's song, "The Wreck of the Edmund Fitzgerald" about "the witch of November come stealin'," and the Beatles' "Something in the Way She Moves," I sat and wrote the piece personifying a blizzard as sinister and calculating.

Contemporary Genius

While reading Aristotle's *Poetics*, I caught myself feeling disappointed that time has destroyed so much art—Homer's comedies, over 100 plays by Sophocles,[32] and even some of Aristotle's own works. But, I thought about all the people I've known who have read great poetry, played great music, showed amazing art to an empty house—tiny crowds and no crowds at all. But people know who the talentless reality spectacles are, along with silly television shows, and that felt like the greater tragedy.

The Elephant Man Crown: Sonnet 1

Before I went to the theatre to see *The Elephant Man* by Bernard Pomerance, I remembered when it came on television in the early 1980s, back when we still had a black-and-white TV with channels we turned with channel lock pliers. That play remains one of the saddest stories I've ever seen.

How could Dr. Treves, the man who saved him—befriended him—later, boil off his flesh and wire his skeleton together for display? Merrick was never a man, just a specimen. It's the loneliest, saddest thing I've ever heard of.

---

[32] *Oedipus Rex* won him second place in the city Dionysia (a large religious festival), by the way, and we think it's amazing. What must his 20 some first-place winners have been like? And who in the world writes more than 100 plays!

So, I researched Merrick's life and wrote a first person point-of-view biopic crown of sonnets, a little symmetry for him at last.

The Craft

Some interesting history about the form is that it originated in 13th century Sicily in the court of Frederick II. There an attorney named Giacomo da Lentino, *il Notaio* (the same Giacomo da Lentino who we find in Dante's *Purgatorio*) wrote the earliest sonnets. Dante, himself, in his *La Vita Nuova*, first used the word we now recognize as "sonnet."[33] The word sonnet actually means "little song."

Scholars theorize[34] that this little poetic form has persisted for so long, and spread to so many countries, due to its representation of a full tone. Many variations on the form exist, but the two most common types are the Italian and the English.

The English sonnet, like the Italian, has an octave, sestet and volta (which we call the "shift" and the "turn" since we speak English).

Observe the alphabetics for each form:

Italian:

A
B
B
A
A
B
B
A
(shift)

C	C	C	C
D	D	D	D
C	E	E	E
D	C	D	C
C	D	C	E
D	E	E	D

(variations of the sestet)

English:

A
B
A
B
B
C
B
C
(shift)
E
F
E
F
(turn)
G
G

---

[33] See *The Penguin Book of the Sonnet: 500 Years of a Classic Tradition in English* by Phillis Levin.
[34] See *The Penguin Book of the Sonnet: 500 Years of a Classic Tradition in English* by Phillis Levin.

Where the Italian seems more static with its divisions at 8 + 6, the English sonnet is much more malleable in where its "shift" and "turn" turn up. Such as 12 +2, (8+4) +2, 8+ (4+2), (4+4+4) +2, (3+3+3+3) +2. The one illustrated, however, is the most common, and its presentation in print is as a single twelve-line stanza (called a *douzain*) with the couplet indented, as I have done with "Contemporary Genius," and "The Elephant Man Crown: Sonnet 1."

In the Italian sonnet, the first eight lines (called the *octave*) set up the situation, and the last six lines (called the *sestet*) offer the resolution, reaction or conclusion. The rhyme scheme for the octave is the chiastic structure of abba, abba. After the octave comes the shift; this is a vital element for the form. The shift in the sestet usually amplifies or refutes what the octave has set up. The rhyme scheme for the sestet can be cdc, dcd or cde, cde.

I Wrote Your Name in the Sand with My Finger

In "I Wrote Your Name in the Sand with My Finger," I have the speaker's lady chasing a gull's feather, and then in the sestet he has "flown" away. As a semicolon would connect two sentences that relate thematically, so too does the octave connect to the sestet.

I modeled this piece after an Italian sonnet,[35] also called a Petrarchan sonnet, named after poet Francesco Petrarch (1304-1374). Petrarch didn't invent the form, but he mastered it so well, it is associated with his name.

My first line alludes to Spenser's "Sonnet 75," "One day I wrote her name upon the strand." A great deal of my audience may overlook this allusion, but those who catch it may find another layer of enjoyment in the work. So it's okay to be subtle; for example, I punned the word *armor* with the Italian word *amore*,

---

[35] I am saying "modeled after" instead of "this is" because I did not write in strict iambs. So technically speaking this is actually *in the style of* a Petrarchan sonnet.

which I know many will miss. Nevertheless, these hidden things add another layer of interest and fun to our writing.

Consider this:

End-rhymes in modern writing are more stylish if they don't sound as hard or obvious as they were in the past. So I tried to make mine as subtle as possible, often going for the assonant or consonant sound like "letter" and "finger."

I did not write in strict meter (iambs, for example), but I did constrict my syllables to 10 per line. Like hard rhyme, strict meter, in my opinion, is out of style.

Confetti of Decay: Sonnet 1

In the opening sonnet for my crown entitled *The Confetti of Decay*, I used an inverted Petrarchan form after Shelley's sonnet "London 1819," as my model. By inverting a form, we can show confusion, or things not being as they should, much as an inverted flag communicates distress.

There's Something in the Way She Screams

I offer this sonnet as an example that is unconcerned with the syllabic count. For this one, I felt more interested in the internal sounds, atmosphere and imagery.

Contemporary Genius

Even in performance, audiences still respond to the sonnet; it has worked for the last 500 years, and it still works. But, often being so dense, some sonnets may be difficult to absorb on the fly. With that in mind and considering that "Aristotle," "Polygnotus," and "Dionysus" are all four-syllable words according to my accent (which use a lot of real estate in a 10-syllable line), I relaxed the count from 10 to 13 syllables in the majority of the poem. Then at the end, the lines expand by one syllable consecutively: 13, 14, 15, 16, 17 counting off like time.

The shift: The octave ends with mention of Ozymandias.[36] From there forward, the piece focuses on time's obliteration of mortal creations.

The turn: I shift again to the immediate shame that we ignore many great, local, contemporary artists.

Also in line 13, I said "town" and not "towns" because I thought "town" felt immediate. "Towns" made it indefinite and dulled the point. This sort of distinction is why we must pay attention to the diction we use. In this same spirit, I left line 2 a syllable short. I could have subbed out "should" for "are to", but I didn't like the sound. It's rare that I'll leave a line out of sync like that, but sound is more important than count. So if you have to choose, go with the music.

Consider this:

I am sure people who fancy that they're "purists" would disagree with changing syllables, or even the number of lines. However, I offer this: meaning dictates form. Form does not dictate meaning. When Gerard Hopkins reduced the sonnet mathematically by ¾ into 10 ½ lines, it was still a sonnet. When Milton added two tercets at the end of a sonnet to create the caudate form, it was still a sonnet. The original sonnets didn't even rhyme. The rhyme word was repeated. Each form has a different rhyme scheme, so the alphabetics don't make a sonnet a sonnet either. Then, it's not the lines, and it's not the rhyme. After a while, it starts sounding like a martini. Every ingredient can change, but it's still a martini. The only thing that makes a martini a martini is the glass.

So, my point is, don't get too uptight about it. Give an artist a rule, and they will show you how to break it. The forms are freedom. They are intellectual exercises with language that invite writers to demonstrate, with mechanisms, things that interest us.

---

[36] "Ozymandias," a poem by Percy Bysshe Shelley (1792—1822), illustrates that even the greatest works, by the mightiest of men, will fall to time. See footnote 28, p.143.

They are paper clips and duct tape, tools, that have been interpreted countless ways with incredible genius.

The Elephant Man Crown: Sonnet 1

This is an English sonnet because Joseph Merrick was English.

I researched what I could about his life and pulled in his own words when possible. "Half-meals," "perfect misery," "not earning my part," were all quotes lifted directly from his autobiography.

Merrick spoke of the beatings issued by his father, so I used that information as a reason for his crippled hip. The solar-white moth serves as something he could distract himself with while enduring the beatings. The moth also symbolized freedom or something heavenly and pure. The "half-meals" Merrick wrote about consisted of turnips and broth, so I added that in as well.

The shift: the octave sets up his situation, and the shift here is an amplification that reveals the lasting severity of the beatings, giving reason for Merrick's crippled hip.

When I saw *The Elephant Man* in the theatre and Merrick said, "Jesus in Heaven makes the crooked straight," I almost felt the sting of tears. (But I didn't! Because I'm so manly I don't weep normal, human tears. I instead weep full-grown rams—one from each eye—that head butt one another to death in a hail of busted rock. So I held back as not to disturb the performance, if but barely.)

Merrick's words are an obvious, yet powerful allusion to Luke 3:5.[37] The allusion stayed with me, and each time I thought of Joseph Merrick, I thought of it. I'd never heard of anyone writing a crown of sonnets to Merrick, and wondered if I would be the first. So in homage to Pomerance's powerful play, I connected my crown to his drama by having my characterization

---

[37] Luke 3:5-- Every valley shall be filled, and every mountain and hill shall be brought low; and the crooked shall be made straight, and the rough ways shall be made smooth.

of Merrick use the allusion as well, though under a different circumstance.

This quote serves as the "turn" of the sonnet. In this case, it's an amplification. As he is beaten, Merrick reminds his father that God watches and one day he will be healed.

Also, I took a cue from W.B. Yeats. In his sonnet "Leda and the Swan," he breaks a line and leaves it hanging to help demonstrate the images of destruction (if you're giving the poem the G-rated reading), pacing it like this: 1. End of a thought. 2. Dramatic pause. 3. New subject shift.

(1)   "The broken wall, the burning roof and tower
(2)   and Agamemnon dead.
(3)   Being so caught up,
          so mastered by the brute blood of the air…"

So in the couplet, I too broke the lines, hedging towards the same effect.

The Invitation

Write out the rhyme scheme of an Italian or English sonnet vertically down the right side of a paper—so the pattern corresponds to the lines ending in rhymes. Skip a line where the shift(s) should occur. Then try some sonnets of your own. Try 10 syllables per line or let them run freely. Find inspiration in feelings, moments or figures from literature, history, or current events.

Beware of the moment when the rhyme tries to change the meaning of your piece. Rhyme is merely a tool. Never change your meaning for the sake of the rhyme; that marks bad writing.

Choose common words and be plainspoken to make your point. Do not comb through a thesaurus in an effort to sound "poetic." It will sound archaic and pretentious at best, or at worst you'll risk looking foolish using a word incorrectly. Either way, your reader is unlikely to think you're brilliant.

Once you have tried a sonnet or two and want an added challenge, try to write a crown. A crown is a series of seven thematically related sonnets that link. The first line of the first sonnet is the last line of the seventh sonnet; the last line of the first sonnet is the first line of the second; the last line of the second is the first line of the third; the last line of the third is the first line of the fourth, and so on. And when these lines are printed, they are generally italicized.

To illustrate:

Sonnet 1, line 1   (italicized)
Sonnet 1 line 14

Sonnet 2 line 1 is sonnet 1's line 14   (italicized)
Sonnet 2 line 14

Sonnet 3 line 1 is sonnet 2's line 14   (italicized)
Sonnet 3 line 14

Sonnet 4 line 1 is sonnet 3's line 14   (italicized)
Sonnet 4 line 14

Sonnet 5 line 1 is sonnet 4's line 14   (italicized)
Sonnet 5 line 14

Sonnet 6 line 1 is sonnet 5's line 14   (italicized)
Sonnet 6 line 14

Sonnet 7 line 1 is sonnet 6's line 14   (italicized)
Sonnet 7 line 14 is sonnet 1's line 1   (italicized)

The difficulty in the first sonnet of a crown lies in representing all the topics and themes that subsequent pieces will address. The first line of the first sonnet is also the last line of the seventh sonnet, punctuating the series.

Consider this:

Speaking of time swallowing great writers, publish your work! I've had too many writer friends pass away and heard that all their great work went straight to the curb, pitched out with the banana peels and coffee grounds like so much trash.

For every Emily Dickinson[38] or John Kennedy Toole[39] who is published, thousands hit the landfill before the light has left their graves.

Submit your own work for publication because no one else will do it for you. There's a business side to writing. Master it.

---

[38] Emily Dickinson (1830-1886) published less than a dozen of her nearly 1800 poems. After her death in 1886, her younger sister Lavinia discovered her writing. Though some of it was published by acquaintances, it was heavily edited. It wasn't until 1955 that a complete, un-edited collection of her poetry was available.

[39] John Kennedy Toole (1937-1969) author of the posthumously published *A Confederacy of Dunces* won the Pulitzer Prize for literature in 1981. After Toole's suicide (from depression over being rejected), his mother championed his manuscript. At last, she showed it to novelist Walker Percy who helped the book to be published.

While the World Decays in Bright Confetti

While the world decays in bright confetti
We charge it confidently unrehearsed
We'll break ourselves long before we're ready

Armed with our comforts and obesity
We shove our neighbors so we might be first
While the world decays in bright confetti

We trick ourselves out for the least money
Then reeling, wonder why we've been so cursed
We'll break ourselves long before we're ready

Some crack cold ones while the rest fall sweaty
Shouting at a roar how they've earned their thirst
While the world decays in bright confetti

Our exhausted cuss the drunk as lazy
And attack the work week at heaving bursts
We'll break ourselves long before we're ready

Gasping on straight whisky or rosary
The hourglass stands for better or worse
While the world decays in bright confetti
We'll break ourselves long before we're ready

The Writer

I wrote a crown of sonnets called *The Confetti of Decay*. From the Shakespearean sonnet in that crown, I pulled the couplet "And the world decays in bright confetti. /We break ourselves long before we're ready," and built my villanelle from that.

The Craft

A villanelle is a nineteen line poem of five tercets (three line stanzas) followed by a quatrain (a four line stanza). The refrain comes from the first and third line of the opening tercet. Then they alternatively end each of the following tercets until coming back together in the last two lines of the quatrain.

To simplify, observe the structure this way. Since the refrains (expressed as R1 and R2) rhyme, I'll define them as A.

Tercet 1)	While the world decays…	(A) R1
	** ** **	(B)
	We'll break ourselves…	(A) R2
Tercet 2)	** ** **	(A)
	** ** **	(B)
	While the world decays…	(A) R1
Tercet 3)	** ** **	(A)
	** ** **	(B)
	We'll break ourselves…	(A) R2
Tercet 4)	** ** **	(A)
	** ** **	(B)
	While the world decays…	(A) R1
Tercet 5)	** ** **	(A)
	** ** **	(B)
	We'll break ourselves…	(A) R2
Quatrain	** ** **	(A)
	** ** **	(B)
	While the world decays…	(A) R1
	We'll break ourselves…	(A) R2

The refrain of the villanelle must build in the work. It is the core of the poem, repeating far too often not to offer anything. In general, repetition emphasizes, so it must push the poem forward.

The all-time worst poem I ever heard at an open mic went for (what seemed like) forty-some lines, each beginning with "Nobody told me... Nobody told me... Nobody told me..." I tried to weave a noose out of bar naps to end the madness. Thank God she finished before I did.

The Invitation

Write the alphabetics down the right side of the page, just like you did on p. 153, indicating where each refrain should be. This will indicate the scaffolding for which you need only apply the content.

This is only an A—B rhyme poem, so choose words for the refrain that you find easy to rhyme. This will free you.

Consider this:

Dylan Thomas' "Do Not Go Gentle Into That Good Night" is probably the most famous villanelle written in the English language. Focus on the word "night." If you wrote a list of rhymes for "night," you could generate quite a few. Look, too, at A.E. Housman's "To an Athlete Dying Young." His first line "The time you won your town the race" ends on a word that rhymes easily (and what an awesome demonstration of iambic pentameter! Observe its ba-Dum ba-Dum ba-Dum ba-Dum meter. If this is something you would like to try, imagine that sound on a click track in your mind, and build sentences that fit to it (rap to it).

You can do this!

THE HALLS OF LEER (A PROVINCE IN HELL I HAVE FOUND)

After many campfires in the Valley of Low,
I ascended Forlorn Canyon's far wall.
At its crest, I came to a fork in the road:
one well worn, the other less traveled

I started down the less traveled road.
It ended in a grotto guarded by a flaming skull
that came to attention and spoke
through a quivering jaw.

> "Abound in darkened halls of Leer
> lurk phantoms, dragons, and visions clear.
> Dungeons cold with dank and stench
> boast strong iron chains and well masoned brick.
>
> No guards, no crowd, no prisoners remain,
> only echoes of terror, axe scars, and stains.
>
> If ever you find that you're in the caverns of Leer
> by dream, or by drug, or meditative sphere,
> escape right away and never return
> lest your soul become branded and doomed to burn
>
> then added to the chorus, added to the screams
> married to the dungeon and tortured by these things!"

If it said more, I'll never know.
I was running two steps behind my inner-coward, inner-child
and stride-for-stride with my feminine side,
                    (not a hair before or behind).

I found the fork and the road more traveled
and raced quickly down it,
learning

that the less traveled road
often leads to a place no one should
or wants to go.

The Writer

Robert Frost's poem "The Road Less Traveled" is so popular and commonly known that it has become clichéd. (To one day be clichéd! If all writers could be so skilled and lucky.).

I may have pulled the title from a dream, but the content is purely fantasy and intended to be a humorous, ironic response to Frost's poem.

I don't always advocate following the crowd, but sometimes they know where they're going. I've gone down a few "less traveled" roads in my day that didn't lead anywhere, that were treacherous or a complete waste of time. The more traveled road may be more traveled for a reason!

The Craft

This type of allusion directly responds to another work. So, "The Road Less Traveled" allusion is introduced right away. The speaker, heeding Frost's advice, heads down the "less traveled" road.

The flaming skull, if ever you see one, should tip you off immediately that things are going poorly.

To differentiate the skull from the speaker, the skull speaks in rhyme. I did this after the witches in Shakespeare's *Macbeth* who speak a more ridged, metered rhyme that emphasizes that they differ from the play's other characters.

The poem ends with a lesson the speaker learned from his travels.

The Invitation

Write responding to other poetry. Use fantasy. Contrast rhyming parts with non-rhyming parts if you like. The tone can be serious or humorous, as I have done. Your poem can make a contradictory point or be sarcastically didactic, teaching the overt.

If you like this kind of writing consider a full parody (if you're poking fun at it):

208

Do you wonder lonely as a smog over a host of wilted daffodils?

Do you not go gentle into that Monday morning?

Do you write an ode to a plastic urn?

Or try a pastiche, if you would more enjoy imitating a work in order to celebrate its characteristics--as in Wordsworth's reverence for nature, or Keats' memorialization of beauty.

Pastiche is an artistic work that imitates another style, work, or period. But not in a way that makes fun of it. That would be a parody.

Pastiche can also be a patchwork, or assembly of pieces to form a literary work.

Double Entry Section

THE EARTHLY TENT DESTROYED

For we know that if the earthly tent we live in is destroyed, we have
a building from God, an eternal house in heaven, not built by
human hands. 2 Meanwhile we groan, longing to be clothed
instead with our heavenly dwelling, 3 because when we are clothed,
we will not be found naked. 4 For while we are in this tent, we
groan and are burdened, because we do not wish to be unclothed
but to be clothed instead with our heavenly dwelling, so that what
is mortal may be swallowed up by life. 5 Now the one who has
fashioned us for this very purpose is God, who has given us the
Spirit as a deposit, guaranteeing what is to come.

2 Corinthians 5:1-5

Here there is darkness,
kidnappings on the border,
murder in Mexico
by men who wear crosses, even tattooed with The Virgin

Deceived by money, doing ultimate evil,
drugged by the power of sending the trapped out
"to see the stars from up close"
as they like to phrase it

When you're cruel it feels better
if you have something catchy and cold to say

Yet for the rest of us tightly bound on our knees
with several guns in our faces
weeping, watching the captors get drunk
before making jokes about how we died

the stars are there like something decent in the darkness
Comfort in the horror

Which reminds us that beyond the earthly tent of our bodies
the clothes and house of Heaven call…
even as we are struck down but not destroyed,
persecuted but not abandoned

That light, racing through the eons to find us
as we brace to go to it
was the first thing God made
the last thing we see

even from a flashing muzzle

SQUINTING OVER BILLS

"It is often safer to be in chains than to be free."
--Franz Kafka

Squinting over bills in the afternoon light
hunched like disappointment has wilted my spine

I drift off into the deep wood-grain print
of the breakfast table where I never eat
because a dining table, even a cheap one
feels too dignified for something
fried to a crust in a microwave

The morning light shines through me
translucent, like I am made of parchment
When I move
I sound like paper
crinkling, flexing, sliding

living in some nightmare of Kafka
I am a bill
made out to myself
from myself
past due

overcharged
and overdrawn

The Writer

The Earthly Tent Destroyed

At the time of the writing, the violence of the Mexican drug cartels was worse than ever. My friends with relatives over the border told me some of their loved ones wouldn't even leave the house anymore.

An article I'd recently read told how one group of killers would joke about taking the victims, at their time of murder, out to "see the stars up close." The fact that they had a catchy line while being evil disgusted me so badly that I wanted to blend it with what I related from 2 Corinthians.

Squinting Over Bills

Barely making bills while working a job we probably don't like feels like some gladiatorial metaphor: fight well in the 9-5 for long enough, earn your freedom with retirement—if you can survive till then.

Once, Discover Card sent me a stack of "convenience checks" and I, feeling rather clever (and being completely busted), paid my Discover Card bill with the "convenience check" they sent. They found it rather inconvenient and would not honor their own check.

I recalled this moment when I wrote: I am a bill/made out to myself/from myself/past due, /over charged/and over drawn.

Depressed and feeling as if I were allowed the grace of life, so I could pay out money to someone else, I directly recalled Kafka's *Metamorphosis* by literally becoming a bill—perhaps another brand of vermin.

The Craft

For Those Who Could Not Write This

The poem opens with "Here there is darkness." I used "darkness" both symbolically and literally. Throughout the stanza, I apply Christian religious iconography to both further the motif established with the quotation and stand as an irony against the actions: evil men tattooed with the Virgin and wearing crosses.

In the second stanza, I added the words "drugged" and "money" as well as the quote I'd heard from the news article about seeing the stars up close. Here, I defined them as in love with money, the root of all evil, and doing the worst of evils.

I continued to reiterate the image of the stars as I added information learned from the article, before I shifted fully into the connection with the quotation. I ended the piece with the image of the flash of light, equating it with the stars and inferring the murder itself.

Squinting Over Bills

The Kafka quote reminded me of the idea that free verse is much more dangerous than formal poetry, as no rules guide the piece. The definitions and the evolution of the work are left entirely up to the writer. But like life, the safety of the shackle is nothing compared to the satisfaction and joy of freedom.

The piece opens with the speaker squinting in the light. As the light hurts our eyes, the bill is also painful. People's backbones are their strength, and this person's backbone is wilted. The character begins to daydream. Here I introduced the surrealistic moment. By the next stanza, the light that hurt his eyes shines through him, piercing him, illuminating him like a parchment. Like Samsa's[40] transformation in Kafka's work, the speaker also transforms suddenly. Instead of the slow tickle of the vermin's legs, I have him demonstrating attributes of paper: crinkling, flexing, sliding.

The Invitation

Write a piece inspired from one of your favorite quotes. If it's from an author, connect the quote with an image from their work and blend it with how you feel about a particular topic.

Or use a current event as your entry point into your writing. Key in on what moved you, and intertwine your ideas with the

---

[40] Gregor Samsa is the antagonist of the *Metamorphosis* by Franz Kafka.

ideas of the quotation and article. Put yourself in the subject's place. Tell the story from that perspective while revealing something about yourself in the process to keep the work feeling authentic.

YOU AND YOUR CAREER

Your career is the headstone where your dreams used to be.

NERVES OF GLASS

Glass jaw
  glass house
    modern man
      well-read mouse.

ON SKIPPING MEALS

I never eat. It messes with my buzz!

WHEN I'M SICK

When I'm sick, I sleep just like the dead (did before they died).

The Writer

Of course out of context, these don't have the pop they do when unleashed well-timed in a conversation. These kill, I swear!

You and Your Career

I don't know what happens to some people, but they can't hold a conversation without going on ad nauseam about their boring job. Or, worse, if you work the same job, they want you to talk about your job, so they can talk about their job and tell you how they do it better. It always feels as if I'm back at work without getting paid or getting anything done. So, I wrote this quote to remind those people who go on about their work world that they don't love that job; they've made friends with it in some twisted display of the Stockholm syndrome. They used to have dreams. I'd rather hear about that.

Nerves of Glass

This guy went off one time calling me a "barbarian." And that may be, but it sounded as if he had created an entire philosophy to justify his own cowardice. This short piece was my response.

On Skipping Meals

This is a deflection I'll use if I'm out and can't afford to eat when friends are ordering up. Humor helps the pain!

When I'm Sick

I get sick once every year or so, and then I completely cave for a day or two. But, I'm a cockroach, man! You can't stomp me out.

The Craft

Metaphor is the prominent mechanism here, but these were obviously just jotted-down, first-draft final-draft writings. Sometimes we just have it.

The Invitation

Write down your own quotable quotes. Next time you're feeling witty and come up with a great zinger or one-liner, capture it in writing.

Of themselves, your zingers and one-liners may not be all that publishable in the printed sense. But, in the going-public-with-your-work sense of publishing, you can drop these one-liners at parties to impress your friends and enrage your enemies. These little beauties may also fit well as a line in dialogue or poetry. They are your banners of life philosophy, your humor and (if you're industrious) a sweet t-shirt.

THIS IS DARKNESS

On the bayou, the fish aren't biting,
and the sky darkens.
The willow I stand beneath tosses its arms,
swaying with the grace of a thin ballerina.

It begins to storm, and I go inside.

Days later, I return and my willow is drowned,
tipped into the rushing current,
arms trailing in the rapids

its neck broken.

The Writer

After reading *One Hundred Poems of the Chinese* by Kenneth Rexroth I felt ready to write one of my own. I used "Stormy Night in Autumn" by Chu Shu Chen[41] as my final inspiration. I intended to write about fishing alone from a muddy bank with only heartache for bait, while watching my bobber fade like happiness, and I reel in the tiniest catfish that does not beg for release; instead, it croaks only *her* name.

It could have been a classic, but it actually stormed that autumn night. When I walked back down to my quiet spot on the bayou, my favorite tree lay uprooted. So, I sat by its mangled remains and wrote this one instead—fashionably depressed, of course.

Much of Chinese poetry conveys a beautifully frank feeling with great economy of language. Characteristically, these poems reveal striking connections between people and the earth developed through the poets' reflection or arriving as an epiphany that arises seamless from the juxtaposition of human and natural images.

The Craft

Many collections of Chinese poetry actually have the original language stamped above the poem. For us who can't read Chinese, it is still interesting to see the block-like regularity of structure, often five characters per line for 4 lines. Our translations usually can't be as orderly, but the scholars do a great job of conveying the beauty of the work, and most often they keep the pieces to just a few stanzas.

So, in my piece, I tried to strike a harmonious balance between the emotional image, the weather and the setting. I also wanted to be as brief as the translations.

---

[41] Chu Shu-Chen was a poet in the 12th century in Hangchow Province. According to the preface written by Wei Chung-Kung in 1182 to a book of her poetry, most of her work was cremated along with her remains after her death, and only a small percentage survived, mostly through oral tradition.

The Invitation

Write using translated poems for inspiration. Read a few Chinese poems, noticing how the writers find tension with their subjects. Then try a two or three stanza poem. In the first stanza, set up a situation in a natural setting (a reflection in a cup, heartache, flies in wildflowers). Then in the next stanza juxtapose something apropos, personified, from the natural world that infers a resolution to the problem (a dreaming candle, the shivering moon behind a cloud, one man missing).

OFFICE OIL PAINTING

In a black frame on the lobby wall,
a man sits on a creek-side rock
looking thoughtful.

A closer look might reveal it's not
a thoughtful look at all
but one of extreme stress and concern

as if his life has just been torpedoed,
and he's beside no creek at all
but a sea of worry where the submarine terrors
of his worst nightmares lurk
and right now his life is an oily shipwreck
with casualties on giant rolling waves
silhouetted as far as the eye can see
beneath a blackness lit only by the full, wide open
and naked eye of Satan

or maybe, I'm just projecting
while I wait for my performance review
with a boss who seems to hate everything
about me.

PORCELAIN COASTER

In sky painted the pale hue of deep ice
even wind is too frozen to bend the tall fan
of eagle feathers set in the warrior's hair.

He may be Crow: his hair is unbound.
The horse he rides dissolves at the hooves
into the earth, and he into the horse.

Calm with war shield slack,
war spear relaxed
traveling alone,

unfazed by the weather
he approaches the demons that whip the tempest
unafraid.

The Writer

Office Oil Painting

The way we feel at a given moment often colors our perceptions of the world around us. Waiting rooms can be nerve-wracking or, at the very least, boring. When I'm a captive audience, awaiting my fate at the dentist's office, administration office, Department of Public Safety, I write.

Often, the art hanging in those rooms barely decorates, but so long as the pieces portray a figure performing some kind of action, I can blend my anxiety or the characters of the other people alongside me to create interesting material.

In this case, I awaited my performance summary. One lesson I learned that year was just because I have a rich cornucopia of expletives, pejoratives, and epithets to call my boss doesn't mean that I should have done it. Believe it or not, it can actually impact the review.

Porcelain Coaster

I have these awful coasters from Oklahoma with truly cool paintings on them. They're awful because they're a heavy porcelain, and the condensation creates a vacuum that welds it to the bottom of the glass. When I pick the glass up to drink, the coaster comes with it, then drops sharply on my foot or hardwood floor, knocking a painful dent into whatever it strikes, and is often followed by long bouts of expletives, pejoratives, epithets and/or my hopping around with deft athletic skill.

But the painted figure riding his horse in such bad weather, with such slack, relaxed posture has always intrigued me. So in spite of the hazards, I keep the few around that I haven't broken to look at when I'm alone and dreaming.

The Craft

From the Greek, *ekphrasis* means to speak out or describe. So ekphrastic poetry, in some way, describes a piece of art. Commonly, it's a famous piece. I've done it in a fairly casual way, here. But I'm a casual guy!

Office Oil Painting

I set up a serene picture of a person fishing, and asked the cliché question: What is he thinking? In reader-response criticism, the reader gets to stand in judgment of a piece, and to see themselves (their history and all their learning and circumstances) reflected in the work. So, here I imposed my own, completely different situation in order to interpret the painting in an outlandish way.

Porcelain Coaster

The harsh conditions and the dignity of the figure have made this piece interesting to me for as long as I've had the coasters; it's a little piece of art I see every time I pick up and set a drink down (so about every forty seconds). At the time of the writing, I read quite a lot of Larry Thomas' poetry (Poet Laureate of Texas 2008). He writes a great deal of ekphrastic poetry, so it made sense to write this one in a way that recalled his style.

The Invitation

Write an ekphrastic poem. Consider a piece of art and try an ekphrastic poem of your own. Use a piece of fine art, commercial art, even a company logo. Give the reader a chance to see the work differently after having read your poem. What do you experience through the art? Share your insight.

BUCKLING LOVESEAT

Where my sawdust-covered, sunbaked body settles
sending cool sighs of rest over blistered hands
muscles untying off the bone.
Where I relax with still empty pockets
sometimes disappointed.

Where my dog crawls up, even when it's a space too small
shedding hair like bags of sticky lawn clippings
on my best clothes, worst clothes.

Here I am an oil painting, rugged and impressionistic
that may only be viewed from beyond the velvet rope
needing a moment of space, with a mind buzzing full of dreams and worry,
a haunt of power tools still roaring in my ears.

The Writer

In my family, a man is measured by his back. My uncle is in his 80s and can still run a chainsaw all day long. My dad can, too. The ability to make and build things is important to us. When I bought my house, I restored the hardwood floors, remodeled the kitchen, and then added a deck and pergola off the back porch.

This poem recalls the day a friend and I hauled many 16-foot long, wet 2x6 boards from the front yard to the back in the 104-degree Houston heat. We then cut and bolted some to the slab and joists and used other boards for the decking and frame and pergola. I even jigged out ogee tips for the decorative pergola top and planted a vine that I had intended to grow up to the top, but it hasn't decided yet if it would rather die or just grow sluggishly.

But, no sooner than we set our tools in the shade, the sun moved and baked them blistering hot. We worked till we were soaked with sweat, stained with sawdust and salt, and deliriously tired for just under two weeks until the project finished.

The Craft

At the time, I read *Electric Light* by Seamus Heaney, and the poem "At Toomebridge" struck me. It wasn't so much the content of the piece, but its sentence structure. Heaney's lines started with the word "where" and kept unpacking and unpacking. It was brilliant, and I had to try it, another pastiche.

The content of the piece reveals pretty much how a person feels after working half to death and needing a moment of silent meditation, undisturbed, unintentionally gruff and spent.

At a line or two, I deviated from Heaney's form because following it perfectly was never the objective.

Consider this:

When you see a syntactical structure you like, take it as far as it's useful for you, but don't let the meaning suffer for the form. When the form needs to change, change it!

The Invitation

Write a poem using another poet's structure. Consider some of the core values in your family: what makes a man a man, a woman a woman, and how do you embody that, or not? Try to capture the demonstrative moment as a poem. If you have an entirely different perspective, then write that.

Our definitions concerning the gender roles of men and women (how they actually are and what we wish they were, what attracts us, and what we need in a match) are so multi-faceted, that this exploration has been the focus of countless works of literature.

SHORT STORY

DEADSHOT RINGING

Stalking the tall grasses of the yard with my one-pump Daisy air rifle and shooting beer cans that passersby littered on our fence line kept me busy for hours. In 1984, at ten years old, I was an expert shot—or at least I thought I was. With no friends for board games and saving Solitaire for after dark and still being unable to read well (with no books in the house but the Bible or literature on vitamins), I pretended that I had to survive alone and abandoned in the bush.

Luckily, the weak air rifle usually only penetrated one side of a can so I could collect and reshoot my rounds. What the cans didn't catch, my grandmother would find with a magnet and save for me in an olive jar. This solid strategy for the resupply of ammunition to my front lines made shooting the eagle from a Budweiser or the "C" from a Coors can mere child's play.

To Dad, we were on hard times, and that's why we lived with my grandparents. I was a soldier, and that never bothered me because no matter how much Dad worked, he always made time to have competitions with me, shooting this tiny thing or that. One day, he shot a locust from way up in the maple tree; my great-grandfather planted that tree, so it was pretty big, and that locust was far off. Dad won that day, and the locust most definitely lost. Dad always won our contests, but I was still pretty strong—an expert if you ask me.

Between the gas station and our house lay a large gravel lot where firecracker stands, vegetable stands and revival tents went up. And when it lay vacant, truckers slept there. This day it was empty.

By 0900 hours, I already had steel on target (because soldiers rise early), and I had shredded every can in my collection to the point there wasn't use in shooting them any longer. The rounds whiffled through striking nothing. Anyway, these were close shots—detail shots—but to be a true expert, a guy has to shoot for distance as well.

Looking to see what I could find, I spied a tire out in the distance, lying in the dust of the gravel lot. I'm not sure exactly how far it out it lay, but I had to peer through the rising heat waves and adjust for gravity, squeezing the round a little high. And if there was a wind, I'd have aimed just slightly into it, using what's known among us experts as "Kentucky windage." But, there was no wind, no clouds—perfect weather for sniping. So I could see the ball lob out through the heat and thump onto the tire. Shot after shot, I sent them down range; each one popping against the target.

After a time, I started thinking that tire looked a might small. I reasoned that maybe it was from a riding mower, but the sound didn't sing with the typical sharp sting a tire usually sounds with, but instead, it rang with a dull pop.

Shouldering my rifle like any world-class sniper—like a professional—I hopped the fence and rolled, reflexively scanned the perimeter, then stalked out to investigate.

About half-way there, I could tell that what I had been shooting was definitely not a tire.

Three-quarters there, the wind blew and stirred its hairs around.

A slow worry settled over me, and against the harsh sun my eyes widened.

Jogging, panic's cold claws crawled in chills up my spine. My worst fears—Tom, my black cat with the gold nugget eyes, the biggest, fattest cat I ever had—the best mouser, the toughest scrapper—the thing that ran half-wild, the same as me lay dead, curled with his mouth partly opened, his jet-black fur dusted white in the chat.

I had been shooting the body of my cat.

I ran back to report, not like a soldier, but like a ten-year-old with horrible news.

Grandfather went to the garage for his concrete shovel and let me show him the body. Being a veteran of many dead pets, he moved with calm, more concerned for my feelings than recovering our fallen friend. The shovel "shushed!" between the gravel and the corpse, and with as much ceremony as one can offer something on a shovel, he carried it back into the yard.

By the porch swing, we had a concrete bird bath, and I guess since Tom hunted there, a powerful sniper in his own right— so often seen as a black streak, in a white froth of water, ripping sparrows off the ledge there—Grandfather though it a fitting headstone.

I remember being amazed at how strong he was at eighty-two that he could so easily move something my child muscles couldn't even budge. And that is where we laid Tom to rest.

Two years later, Grandfather was laid to rest, five years later Grandmother laid to rest too, and that tiny house sold. For twelve-thousand dollars.

Still, all these many years later, that yard holds the rusted BBs, a cat and the memories of a man who was once an expert marksman.

The Writer

Since we lived on a busy road, people stole our dogs, our lawnmowers, and constantly littered cans in our yard. I had a one-pump Daisy air rifle, and I was awesome with just the iron sights. Grandmother would pick up the beer cans, and I would shoot them. Then she would look around for my BBs with a magnet and put them in a jelly jar, and I'd shoot them all again.

These cans were such a fact of life that we decided we'd collect them for the aluminum. We even went to the stock car races where my aunt worked to pick them up. We saved. We hoarded. When I got in trouble, instead of whipping or grounding me, Dad handed me a sledgehammer, and I'd have to go smash cans—spraying myself with all the nasty mold and stale beer.

We had black garbage sacks full of cans piled over one another and filling our garage until we finally took them in to the recycling plant and made twelve bucks per bag. That ended that. No more collecting cans. But it didn't end the shooting.

My dad actually did shoot a locust out of a tree, and I really did shoot a tire that turned out to be my dead cat.

When I went into the Army, I continued to be a good shot. Actually, one of my few regrets about my service is that my DD Form 214[42] records me as only scoring Sharpshooter[43] because I didn't understand that I had the responsibility to update it after each requalification.

The Craft

Characterization is merely a set of rules writers give to people in a story. These people are revealed by direct characterization (which tells the audience what a character is like), and indirect characterization (which shows what the character is like). It's within these parameters (of both attributes and flaws) that writers

---

[42] DD Form 214 contains the complete, verified record of a person's military service and includes all pertinent service information, including awards and medals, promotions, training, etc.
[43] The marksmanship ratings for the Army are Marksman (24 of 40), Sharpshooter (29 of 40), Expert (36 of 40).

decide their behavior. The protagonist here is a child who likes to pretend he's an amazing sniper. So, to make him more credible, I had him speak in military lingo and use the 24-hour military time. I wanted to build it up as if he actually considered himself a sniper.

Cats are generally solitary hunters, so too are snipers, and so is this character who most often plays alone.

Consider this:

When writing about yourself, it's generally best to create a version of you that you can hurt or make to look like a fool—a caricature of yourself with rules for behavior just the same as a completely fictional character. If it's too much exactly like you (or so you think), your character runs the risk of being treated too preciously, being portrayed too pitifully or too amazingly.

Forestalling a philosophical dissertation questioning the exact nature of truth, let me say, don't feel overly bound by the exact facts when writing about yourself. A little fiction can lubricate a true story just enough to make it work. Readers do not need blow-by-blow descriptions and a dozen backstories to experience your telling. Keep it succinct. Use poetic devices and literary techniques.

The Invitation

A great quote by Ernest Hemingway is etched on a silver pen box my mother gave me: "The writer must write what he has to say, not speak it."

Childhood memories provide excellent opportunities for writing. So next time you find yourself retelling an old story, take note. Follow Hemingway's advice, and write it.

236

THE WHEELIE

The first thing Anna Marie Wineshank didn't realize was that I was a daredevil—one of the best curb jumpers and bunny hoppers in Tulsa, Oklahoma, according to my two friends which was awful impressive. The second thing she missed—and maybe she missed a lot of things—was me.

Dad bought my first bike after saving like crazy, but I only rode it twice before it got stolen by an older kid from the sixth grade, and that liked to have killed my soul. Nice things need good locks, I guess. We caught my second bike while catfishing on the Arkansas River; it wasn't near as nice, being rusted-out with no seat or tires, but Dad fixed it up and it became my life—way better than a catfish, if you ask me.

The first time I saw Anna Marie, the air hovering just over the street shimmered with heat as she rounded the hilltop. And she'd glide, ever so delicately, from her neighborhood through mine most every day.

After school, I'd ride my bike hard to get home in time to hide inside, out of sight, and gaze out at her from the picture window. Even through the dusty droplets of dried rain on the window glass, she looked like some kind of angel on a 10-speed. Slow as a drifting cloud, she would coast by, tick-tick-ticking along. I don't ever once recall her pedaling. It was as if the street just brought her along, ever so gently.

Days like this went by, and a body could say that I had it bad. I guess I was in love, or at least in crush. The record player in my brain stuck, playing only one name: Anna Marie Wineshank. Anna Marie Wineshank. Anna . . . I had to introduce myself.

In the quiet of the bathroom, I tried on different lines, looking cool in the mirror, hoping to catch one just suave enough to use. I combed my hair out of my eyes and everything.

"Hello, Anna Marie. I've been admiring you from afar." No, too direct.

"Anna Marie, I'm Craig. Pleasure to acquaint with you." That was nice—sounded high-class. Maybe I should play it cool. How about, "They call me Craig, Anna Marie. They call me that because it's my name. What about you and me do a lap around the block together—just the two of us?"

Maybe I needed a hat.

One Saturday, I was out pulling off some really gutsy daredevil stunts, jumping curbs, popping wheelies, wearing my favorite red running shorts, sleeveless mesh half-shirt and extra-long red-and-yellow striped tube socks pulled straight up to my knees. I saw her tick-tick-ticking towards me over the hill. My love angel surprised me!

My face flushed red. My heart popped a wheelie, and I freaked out, scrabbling around in the dirt track of my mind for just one of the cool lines I'd practiced—anything! I couldn't even find my voice.

I wanted to give her some roses and chocolates, but I didn't have any money. I thought about inviting her inside for a sandwich, but we were down to the heels. My throat dried up; I was finished.

I was going to have to resort to amazement. She would need to feast her eyes on something so cool, so spectacular, she couldn't help but pedal over to congratulate me on a job well-done.

Culvert ditches to the left and right of the street were deeper than any other I'd ever seen. I would speed down the hill like a madman headed for the dangerous ditch on one side, then cut out sharply just before the drop-off and ride a wheelie. Then I'd race over to do it again on the other side of the street, weaving to the right, to the left, and back to the right. Then, a few feet in front of her, I'd wait coolly for her to tick-tick-tick on over to me, her new daredevil hero. It was dangerous, but this is when a man has to dig deep, and I was all in.

I involuntarily screamed as I shot downhill toward her, pedaling hard. She looked a little startled, but I was about to be amazing, so it didn't matter. I swerved dangerously close to the ditch, popped up, and rode a short wheelie, not my best, but I dashed over to the other side of the street to try again.

I cut in toward the ditch, swerved out, and popped up again. Suddenly, I saw my lousy front tire shoot off, flying up above the hill and rapidly shrinking as it sailed out into the distance. Horrified, I felt the forks of my bike bite into the street, throwing sparks like some kind of firework, jolting me up into a handstand over the handlebars. For part of a second, it had to look beyond cool. Then I slapped against the concrete. My palms lit up with pain, and if I could have thrown sparks, I might have as I slid, skinning myself with only a mesh half-shirt to protect me. My tube socks fell down, and I tumbled right off the road into the tall weeds of the ditch, gulping like a landed catfish, groaning like I was half dead.

"Anna," I called hoarsely. "Anna, my darling. I'm … fine …."

But she didn't hear. Maybe I was entirely hidden in the weeds. The closest she came to helping me was when her shadow floated over my quavering body like the comforting hands of an angel, as she went tick-tick-ticking by, never once stopping to make acquaintance with me—or even what was left of me.

The Writer

For this story, I cobbled together a few memories. Here's the truth:

My grandfather used to walk me to school every day, but he was in his 80s. One day, he got lost coming home. From then on, I had to walk myself. When I reached the third grade, my dad saved money and bought me a Raleigh Rampar 400, my first brand-new bicycle. Instead of making the long walk alone, I could ride. I loved my bike for two weeks, two glorious weeks. Then a sixth grader snatched my cheap lock with such force, he busted it. He stole my bike right off the front rack at school.

My first betrayal. I couldn't believe someone would do that—given what that bike meant, how hard it was for Dad to save.

I would have given anything to find that boy, to savagely whip him flat to the ground, with a busted fan belt like I had whipped the other bully a few weeks prior, but he was long gone.

So, I cried all the way home, unashamed about who saw me.

When I came in, and Dad heard what happened, he went out looking for my bike. And he tracked down who did it, and saw it upside down in the guy's yard, spray painted all black and ugly to disguise it, but the police told him he couldn't do anything. So... that was that.

Sometime later, my step-dad caught a bike frame while catfishing. He stripped it all down, painted it blue and surprised me with it. It was a great bike. We bought a better lock, and I took it everywhere.

I learned to ride a wheelie on that bike. My grandparent's house sat on a slight hill, and I would ride wheelies all the way down to the dead end, and race back up. Except, one time, as I popped up, my front tire flew off, and I wiped out. That cost me three stitches in my chin.

Four years later, once Dad re-married, we moved to some duplexes. I liked a beautiful girl who lived in the nearby neighborhood. She was much older, and I didn't exist. However, the idea stuck in my head that if she only knew about my amazing bicycling skills, she would be mine. I had to impress her.

I wore the uniform of 1985: a mesh half-shirt, short shorts and tube socks pulled up to my knees. I swooped in cutting my wheels left and right. I began to amaze even myself... until I hit some gravel and splashed onto the street, earning a road rash that pretty well covered my miserable, nearly naked body, except for where the mesh half-shirt protected me. My chest and belly looked like a sack of apples in white mesh, the rash bleeding through in a decorative lattice.

She didn't even stop to see if I lived...I lay flat out, recovering as her 10 speed clicked off into the distance. That marked the very last time I ever tried to be cool.

My character's love interest borrows her name from a girl I went to 5th grade with. She never spoke to me either.

When this story originally was published in *Cowboys and Indians Magazine*, the real Anna saw it and sent a letter saying she knew that I had used her maiden name because it was so unusual. I wrote her back to say my character only borrowed her beautiful name, but she was off the hook for the actions because a different girl had left me crumpled in the ditch.

The Craft

Since the bike was caught while fishing and the character wore a mesh half-shirt (which recalls a fish net), I used that as a subtle metaphor, blending it with his being a daredevil.

When I characterize Anna, I describe her as an angel. She floats. The road pulls her along as if she's on a cloud. This contrasts her (an angel) to him (a daredevil).

With these as my guiding metaphors, I describe actions in the story in terms consistent with these metaphors. Instead of using the cliché "My heart was in my throat!" or "My mind went blank!" I have my character say, "My heart popped a wheelie, and I freaked out, scrabbling around in the dirt track of my mind for just one of the cool lines I'd practiced."

You might comb your draft looking for clichés and redefining them according to metaphors you've already established. This will offer a continuity to your work and reinforce the subtle motifs and themes you have working.

I let the audience be the more-knowing observer as my young character worries over how he might impress Anna. And when he is too poor to get her flowers or is hurt on the road, I never have him complain. That would break the humor and the sympathy. I leave him optimistic and blissfully ignorant. The audience will naturally recall their own lives and feel empathy for the character.

Consider this:

It is better to apply what you know with show versus tell on the larger scale, certainly, but do it with the smaller details as well. When my character looks out the window, I, as the writer, looked out the window too, and described the water stains on it. The small details will give a feeling of reality to the work as well as further illustrate your character.

The Invitation

Write a humorous story. Writing in a manner that allows us to laugh at ourselves is a great way to enter a story. How have your attempts to be impressive gone?

Look for and encourage the natural themes already inherent in your stories, as I did with the catfishing and daredeviling.

As you write, you may need to use a cliché to keep the pen moving, but as soon as you can, go back and revise it out. Reconstruct more colorful descriptions instead that work logically with your metaphors and themes.

242

Brave, Clean, and Reverent

Decembers in Oklahoma kept me indoors straddling the grate of the floor furnace, staring down through its little round window at the flickering blue pilot light; my coat was just too thin to spend much time outside. We didn't take cable television or have sweets to snack on. With Dad sick and Mom sleeping all day and working nights to provide all that we had, they weren't much entertainment. A guy could go right out of his mind with boredom, but not me! I had the Cub Scouts, and they were the best thing in my life. I was a Webelo. I knew the handbook by heart and had almost every badge but the Arrow of Light, and I was working on that.

It was coming near Christmas time, and I volunteered to do a fundraiser to buy winter clothes and presents for disadvantaged kids. I used to have a neighbor friend that was disadvantaged like that. I knew because his mom said she didn't have money for a shirt he liked at the Goodwill, and even my mom had money for that. She got me clothes there once a year and some were awful nice.

For my fundraiser, I had a cardboard suitcase of treasures to sell. I had pot holders, refrigerator magnets that would hold a picture, spoons for stirring, whisks for mixing, key chains, doilies, compasses and gadgets galore. More treasures than I could hardly believe.

I put on my uniform—it was clean—cinched up my neckerchief, and took my suitcase out into the frosted afternoon. I began working the neighborhood; I wrote a sales pitch and everything.

My first house was Mr. Johnson's across the street. His front yard was blacktopped, and he worked on old cars there. I don't believe I ever saw him get one running, but he sure had their greasy parts spread out like he might.

The door opened, and I began: "I'm in the Cub Scouts, and I'm selling…"

"No thank you," the woman interrupted. "Mr. Johnson has passed away. We are in mourning."

"I liked Mr. Johnson," I said, feeling sad.

"No trinkets for us," she said. Her hot words made a little fog of breath before the door shut.

I went to the next house. It looked like somebody's dog had torn open the side of their white trash bag to get at the chicken bones. After I knocked, someone peeped out at me for a good few moments before the door opened.

I said, "I'm in the Cub Scouts and ..."

"No thanks." And the door shut.

"Dogs aren't supposed to eat chicken bones," I said.

The blinds bent and someone peered out at me, and from the other side someone shouted, "Beat it!"

"Don't you like being helpful?" I shouted back. Then just to show him what's what, I picked up his nasty trash bag and put it all back in his can where it belonged. Then I moved on to the next house.

I hit every address on my block and sold three things. I had no idea I was such a silver-tongued salesman. Half-frozen, I had just one house left—the house I skipped. The most dreaded house in the world: Tony and Irene Tulsa. Their house sat sort of crooked. Their fake shutters were missing slats or missing altogether. In the frost, it looked like the gingerbread house of someone who hates gingerbread. They scared me to death. It wasn't anything they said or did. It was that they were different. They were a family of dwarves, and they were very small.

I stood at the curb looking up the cracked sidewalk to their house—which was nicer than mine, really; they kept their hedge trimmed and everything. But I lost my nerve. I was too afraid to knock and, disappointed in myself, turned to leave.

The front door cracked open, and Mrs. Tulsa stepped forward, her small body braced against the wind. Almost mechanically, I said, "I'm in the Cub Scouts, and I'm selling treasures for your kitchen and home. May I show you what luxuries I offer?" I wrote that spiel myself and considered it quite slick.

"You're the boy from up the street."

"Yes, Ma'am."

"I've seen you playing catch by yourself in the front yard," she said. "Don't you have any friends?"

"Would you like to see my treasures? I'm selling them to raise money for disadvantaged kids."

I don't know why, but hearing that she smiled and said, "Will you come in? You're shivering."

I could hear the point of my neckerchief whipping with the wind—maybe like Superman's cape. Maybe like a newspaper on a phone pole.

Miss Tulsa waited patiently, smiling at the door.

It wasn't easy, but Scouts are supposed to be brave, though I didn't feel brave just then. But I smiled at her as best as my cold face would allow and trudged up their sidewalk and went inside.

I lay my suitcase down and opened the lid. She knelt with me on the old hardwood of their living-room floor and together we picked through it. I explained the benefits of owning each of my sturdy gizmos. I was still pretty nervous, until Tony came in from the other room; then Irene made us all hot chocolate. This relaxed me a lot, and really warmed me up. With the heat of the warm mug against my cold hands while I watched the three tiny marshmallows floating around inside, I decided their home was very comfortable.

"I like your name," I told her. "Irene sounds like *ire* which means anger, but your last name is Tulsa, and that means peaceful. It's cool."

"I think it actually means old town," she said.

"Well, that's okay," I said. "I still like it." Then I told her my name was Craig, and that meant *rock*: from the crag and strong. I didn't know how true it was, but it meant better than it might have.

Tony was an artist who made furniture from horns and driftwood. I could hardly believe some of the things he made. This was his busiest time of the year with people buying so many of his treasures for gifts. The rest of the year, they traveled to powwows and trade shows—

door-to-door sales, kind of like what I was doing for my fundraiser.

Then I told them all about scouting. They didn't ask about my family, and I was glad. Maybe they could tell I'd just rather not bring it up. I stayed for I don't know how long, and when it was time for me to go, I asked if they would be buying anything today. Irene looked at Tony, and he got the checkbook. They bought nearly everything in my case. I couldn't believe it. I thanked them for being so nice to me and boxed up the remainder of my things. When I reached for the door, Irene said, "Did you get your coat?"

"No, ma'am," I said. "It's so thin I don't even bother with it. Besides, I wanted to show off my uniform."

"Are you going to any more houses today?"

I shook my head no. "You were the last."

"Wait a moment," she said and went round the corner. I heard hangers scraping on a rack, and she brought back an army field jacket.

"Take this. It was my brother's."

"Won't he need it?" I asked.

"He can't use it anymore. And look, it's too big for me!" she said laughing. "Take it."

I put it on, and it felt great. It was a little big for me too, really, but way better than the flimsy thing I had at home. And I know better than to refuse a nice gift. People think that's rude.

Tony invited me back to watch him work sometime and maybe even help.

I couldn't believe how great they were—the nicest people in the neighborhood, and I had some money for my fundraiser. When I stepped out in the chilly wind with my new coat on, I thought about how lucky the disadvantaged kids were going to feel when they get their new coats and presents. Maybe, like me, they'll even be able to play outside a while. I guess my good deed lit a pilot light that started flickering around somewhere in the floor furnace of my heart, because it warmed me right up from the inside out. And I could tell the Tulsas felt really good about supporting us Cub Scouts and making a new friend, too.

The Writer

Across the street and a few houses down lived a family of little people. In truth, I never knew their names. But, I was always afraid of them. So, when I knocked on their door with my Cub Scout uniform on and my cardboard suitcase in hand, and they welcomed me with such generosity, I felt like a goat. They actually did buy almost everything I had.

All my life I regretted fearing and judging them because they were different. I wanted to write this piece in penance.

Since this piece would publish in the Christmastime issue of *Cowboys and Indians Magazine*, I took advantage of the "dwarf" allusion and wrote Tony Tulsa as a craftsman, or maybe he was supposed to be an elf. (I hope that admission doesn't make me a goat all over again.)

Though I accurately described the street, the guy who lived in the house with the ripped trash bag in his front yard was actually a little more sinister than I wrote him here. And it was a black trash bag in the back behind his fence.

His house lay two down from mine. For years, an elderly, cotton-haired lady lived there. I never saw her dressed any way but in a nightgown, even during the day. She shared a party line with us—and she loved to talk on the phone.

Grandmother said that the woman discovered her son was living on the streets, and she took him in. But soon after he began living there, the lady died. She had a big, white German shepherd and a male mallard duck that ran her yard. I could always see the dog and hear the quacking duck. Then the dog came up dead, and after a while, I no longer heard the duck, either.

My friend—whose family rented the house next door—and I were out shooting BB guns in a small alley behind our row of houses. We saw a black trash bag in the weeds behind the old woman's fence. Being young explorers, and curious kids, we opened it. A whoosh of putrid air rushed out, billowing from the sack, the most hideous smell of rotted flesh, right in our faces. We dumped the sack, and out rolled the mallard with a human bite mark in the side of its neck.

After that, we threw rolls of toilet paper in his yard. A pitiful vengeance that lay there until the rain and the sun turned the paper to pulp, and the pulp to earth.

The Craft

The prominent mechanism in this piece is inference. The character doesn't realize he is the disadvantaged kid, but the Tulsas (and of course the readers) do. This is dramatic irony. As writers, we can have our characters not know things that other, more sophisticated characters and the audience know.

Because he could at least go to Goodwill once a year, he considered his friend "disadvantaged" as his friend could not. And to increase sympathy for the character, I had him playing catch (a two-player game) alone. But the entire effect would have failed if he had ever said, "Man, I'm poor. I am so disadvantaged!" He had to remain unaware, even to his closing remarks.

The audience constantly makes judgments as they read. Good writers leave space for them, room within the scenes, to make their own minds up. This is how active readers participate.

And this is why showing is so much more powerful than telling in a scene.

The coat symbolized the character's poverty. His situation made room for the symbol to appear. In this case, the weather I created made his best coat so insufficient he doesn't even use it. Then I reinforced that symbol by keeping him in the cold (to demonstrate his need for a coat). Then I did it again when Irene gave him her brother's coat, and again when he felt proud about how he would help other disadvantaged kids get new coats, too.

Once you create a symbol, spiral it through the work to increase its meaning.

Also, by Irene saying, "It was my brother's," and "He can't use it anymore," I was able to further use the inference that her brother had passed away, possibly through military action, as it is a military coat. Readers notice this, but the character does not.

For the stories involving a caricature of myself, I like to use first-person point-of-view. By its nature, first person is limiting, so it lends itself well to blissful ignorance. This character's wisdom does not match his situation. He is an unreliable narrator. The character learns, for the first time, lessons that the older, more experienced reader has known for a while.

> First person singular point-of-view is a narrative told by a character who speaks about themselves.

Consider this:

This character has a certain voice, a way of phrasing. I can hear him talking in my mind as I write; I hear the words he says in his voice. Each character should have a unique voice in the mind of the writer, and just as people in life have idiosyncratic ways of speaking (idioms and phrasing), so should our story people. However, avoid writ-in lak dis tu git dial-ects, as much as possible. Misspellings like this for dialects can work (such as in *Their Eyes Were Watching God* by Zora Hurston), but they usually look insulting or are off-putting due to the difficulty of deciphering them.

The Invitation

Write for atonement. Is there something in your past that you would like to apologize for through literature?

Use that story as an opportunity to create a character who is unaware of his or her own situation (as you likely were), and work with the idea of inference.

> Dialogue tags denote which character is speaking. For example, "Get busy writing that story," Chris said.

Were you upset that someone couldn't come out to your event, but didn't realize they suffered from a private illness? Were you hurt by someone's seemingly cheap gift but didn't know it meant something special? Do you look back on a portion of your life and joke about not knowing how poor you were?

Set up situations in which the more-knowing reader will clearly see what the character cannot. Consider a first-person telling, and work with idioms and phrasing to give your characters voices that sound unique to them. This will also relieve some of the burden from the dialogue tag.

Even Ironwood Rusts

The baby had us all up well before daybreak. Kelley and I fussed with making meal mush and bacon which usually worked to settle him down. Since three teeth came in, he'd chewed off the tops of all his bottles. He was practically born with teeth and seemed to keep a secret that, if he thought on long enough, whipped him into an uncontrollable rage.

Grandfather sat in his wheelchair, unbothered, quietly staring through the picture window bathed in the light and buzz of the street lamp, listening to the cats fight.

Virgil, our cat, only came in long enough to eat and wouldn't tolerate more than a stroke or two before he began screaming for the street. The indoors seemed to kill his soul—he lived to hunt and fight and roam the night, and he did so with the most primal ecstasy I'd ever seen in any other living thing. My grandfather loved him.

Twenty-five years ago a stroke paralyzed Grandfather's left side, but he still dragged himself around with a walking cane, resisting the wheelchair until a fall broke his femur off at the ball, and the surgery paralyzed his bladder. So now he sat in a wheelchair, barely speaking anymore at all, plugged into a catheter that's contents swung in a discreet satchel beneath the chair.

With the baby in one arm, Kelley stirred the mush and asked, "Are you going to talk to the neighbor about cutting his limb off our house? It swept off a bunch of shingles after the storm the other night."

"I went over on Monday," I said, "and told his wife I'd like to talk to him."

"Monday?" she said, "That's three days gone. He's avoiding you."

I poured us each a cup of coffee and said, "Maybe he's been busy."

She shook her head. "You scared him. Ever since he saw you busting concrete with the sledge that day you lost your temper on the contractors."

"The ones who broke our flower box?" I asked. "They deserved it for being smug. And don't act like you aren't glad I said something. If you'd have gotten there first, it would have been a lot worse. Trust me."

"Russ is a timid sort," she said. "You have to take it easy on him."

"His old tree is falling apart," I said. "Once it was the prize of our block, but now the limbs it drops are getting bigger and bigger. I'd cut the thing myself, but it's too high for me to reach."

"Things die," she said. "They get old. They can't stay strong forever." She turned the bacon, and as it quivered and popped, I saw a drop of hot grease bite her on the arm. She rocked back, as if to check that the baby wasn't struck, but otherwise gave no sign of pain. "You have to leave that trimming to a professional."

"In Gramps's time," I said, "men got out and did that sort of thing themselves. And if a tree was beating up a neighbor's house a guy got an apology. He didn't have to ferret out a man from hiding to get it fixed."

Kelley said, "All men don't have boxers and war veterans for grandfathers. People are different, and I say you scared him. So be easy."

In the other room we heard grandpa laugh, and since that was such a rare sound anymore, we all looked in. Through the window, outside, we saw a big white cat dart from the hedge and sprint across the street. Virgil walked out calmly behind and sat down in the light of the street lamp. He licked his paw and ran it once over the bloodied tip of his ear. That white cat had whipped Virgil for months; tonight it ended.

I clanked the plates and silverware onto the table. Kelley put the baby down on the small carefully quilted blanket so she could bring breakfast. But before she had turned two steps away, he had crawled off across the room and sat down beside the large wheel of grandfather's chair—where together they remained silently watching the final moments of darkness before the dawn.

The Writer

Most of the instances in the story are true, except for the baby. My actual grandfather never had the chance to make it to my house for a visit, so I brought him home in story.

In this piece, I wanted to explore the idea that each character is at tension and in his or her own cycle of life. To find the elements, I blended situations and characters from my real life beginning with a central issue: the tree.

The Craft

If we imagine that within the five rays of a pentad there are more pentads in a Fibonacci sequence, we may consider how Shakespeare wrote Osric in *Hamlet*. This character has such a small part, but Shakespeare still gave him an interesting psychology. Nobody is wallpaper with Shakespeare. So, if each ray of the pentad represents a concept, and the drawing represents the drilling deeper into each one, writers can map the various elements of their story to conceptually "drill down," discovering greater meaning and tension.

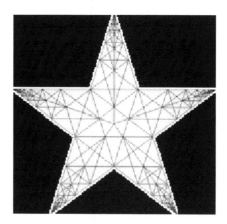

With this concept in mind, I set up contrasts in each character's arc of life—even with items from the setting such as the tree and the bacon; the man and wife, the baby, the grandfather and the cats—everybody had an issue to contend with.

It gave a stronger atmosphere to the story. Everything exists at tension.

As one night ends, a new day begins. The tree, once strong, now is failing; Grandfather was strong yet nears the end of life; the grandson is at tension with the neighbor; the white cat lost to Virgil that night.

Consider how the story would have suffered if I had left this technique out, never "drilling down" into the characters and only focused on the conversation between the speakers. The impact would have felt considerably weaker and rested solely at the surface.

Consider this:

The word "protagonist" broken down from the Greek means "the one in agony" or at struggle. The antagonist is the force against him. This conflict is usually defined in the following ways:

> character vs. character
> character vs. nature
> character vs. society
> character vs. fate/God/universe/luck
> character vs. technology/science
> character vs. self

Conflicts may blend, but there should be a dominant one. Here, the dominant conflict is with the neighbor (character vs. character).

I enjoyed writing about the woman cautioning her husband about his temper, then adding tension by implying (through the man's comments) that she is much more dangerous than he is— which we see when the bacon sparks her arm and she has no reaction other than to check the baby. Of course, cooking bacon and holding a baby is obviously ill-advised, but that, too, adds to tension. In real life, nobody is a model parent. Why would our story people do everything correctly?

The Invitation

Write considering the quality of your conflict and tension.

Imagine two stories.

Story 1. Everything is perfect.

Story 2. Everything is perfect, until it isn't.

Story 2 is more interesting. It invites questioning: What's not perfect? Why?

To have an interesting story, we must have conflict and tension.

In your story, look at the quality of your conflict. Is it clearly defined, and are there subordinate conflicts that complement it? Remember the pentad with the Fibonacci pattern, and give each character (and major items of a scene) a conflict or a tension. Like Shakespeare, consider that nobody is wallpaper, and the setting contributes to theme and characterization.

THE YEAR OF THE RAKE

It was the sort of road where something dead, or dumped, always lay splattered along the shoulder. This morning it was a skeletal thin, brown horse. It probably never worked or raced or did anything but waste away in some filthy cubicle until last night when, finally, it slipped into the darkness escaping a lifetime of misery. It sprinted, excited by the heavy sounds of its drumming hooves on the crumbling road before it stumbled and dropped dead near junk houses and stacks of bald tires with its innards exploded out of its rectum. This was the route I took to work. And the mess of it looked like I felt about my job.

At the end of each day, I stood in the office at the sign-out clipboard after everyone else had gone, multiple phones ringing, lines flashing unanswered. The lid to the aquarium had fallen in; several fish, belly up with their eyes pecked out rested near it, moving a little on the bottom, pushed around by the bubbles from the aerator gurgling in a sliver line behind. And that would be my last image of the day. Then, for the entire drive home, I would try to imagine that my own silver lining wasn't far behind. It was a meditation. I had to hope that out there, somewhere, karma or the Universe or God would listen and grant me a little justice. It was all I had left.

Mr. Trudgwic waited, holding a white slip when I came into work last Tuesday morning. He was smiling. "Mr. West, it seems you're moving a bit slow on that last work order."

"The one from Friday?" I answered.

He paused, his bug eyes flashing as if he were considering what a fantastic idiot I had to be for asking. "Yes."

I said, "I stayed until 9:30 the last two nights working in the storage closet. Everything is so disorganized back there I can hardly find what I need. Whoever is handling the orders is just dumping things in there."

"Humm humm," he said.

I continued, "And Thursday I had to help the secretary with the order for the new security cameras. The vendors are new, and she doesn't yet know how to code them. I'll get it done today, sir, before I leave."

I tried to call him "sir" every now and then to soften him up, though it rarely worked.

He pushed the white paper in front of me. "Indeed you will, Mr. West. Here's a reminder to see that you aren't late again."

"Are you serious, another disciplinary form? But the project isn't even late! I have three days yet before the deadline."

"It's a written and oral directive that when projects run into the following week you are to notify your superior of its status. I was not notified... sir."

"As long as the deadline is met, what's the difference? I never miss a deadline."

He shook his head. "Mr. West, it's a written and oral directive. If you need help complying with the policy, reach me in writing, and I will see that you are properly assisted. Now, if you please, sign on the line, unless you refuse. I have other duties to attend."

I paused, stunned. In eleven years with the company I'd never been written up, ever, for anything, and suddenly with this supervisor I'd been through it three times now for nickel-and-dime infractions: three minutes late after gridlock traffic following a fatality accident, not signing out after working late, not signing an absence-from-duty form after a piece of equipment fell on my head giving me the mother of all headaches.

It seemed the more he wrote me up, the better supervisor he thought he appeared to be. I was at the point that I expected it now, like some Pavlovian response, and each meeting concluded with a warning of "assistance" to help me comply with the policy. Every encounter ruined my entire evening. I need this job. I have a lot of self-esteem wrapped up in it. I've been at it for eleven years, how could I not? I'm the sort of person who prides himself in the work I do. Now, I go home, drink a six pack and fall asleep. It's all I have the energy for. Maybe it's all I'm good for.

In years past, I was called the company's best tech. I'd been employee of the year, head of my department, developed and lead trainings. Now, I was apparently incompetent.

The next morning, on Friday, he came at me again with another white piece of paper. "Mr. West, it seems you forgot to sign out last night."

I groaned.

"Excuse me, was that disrespect I just heard?"

"Sir, I worked late," I said. "When I left, the office was locked. There weren't even any custodians around to let me in. And, I thought only the sign-in sheets were auditable documents, not the sign-out."

He chuckled as if he pitied my response. "Excellence is our standard, sir. Working late is never an issue, and I applaud you for your extra efforts, but when we leave it is vital that we adhere to policy. It is a written and oral directive."

"What harm did I do?" I asked.

"It is vital" he repeated, "that we adhere to the standards. Sign here, please, unless you refuse." He looked as if he would like nothing more than for me to refuse. "And if you need assistance complying…"

"I got it," I said. "Let you know, and you'll assist me."

"It's almost like you read my mind. Good day."

As he walked off, I stood there looking after him, feeling trapped. This had once been a great place to work. I took the lead on extra projects, donated unpaid hours, and we were outperforming other branches. Really on the rise. Then he took over. Now, I never ask for extra duties, and life here has never been worse.

I took my write-up and went back to my small office room to check my work tickets. Mr. Trudgwic had sent an order to take down his security camera. We were going from black-and-white to color. It was a building-wide upgrade and quite expensive. He, of course, wanted his replaced first.

I got my toolbox and headed towards his office, which felt like the longest walk I'd ever made. The hall seemed to stretch on forever. My blood pressure went up. My mouth went dry, and I hoped he was away bothering someone else, but he wasn't. He was standing at the four-way hall, right by his office, watching everything with those huge, bulging eyes of his.

I bent my head low and tried to slip by without him acknowledging me.

"Mr. West! Glad you could find the time. You're here for the upgrade, I assume?"

"Yes, sir."

"Excellent. But where is the replacement? I see that you've brought nothing but tools."

"The delivery truck hasn't arrived. It should be here today."

His happy look soured into one of disapproval. "So, I'll be without a camera then, for how long?"

"A couple of hours, probably." I moved past him and began dismounting the camera.

He forced a smile back and tried to seem friendly. Socially, Mr. Trudgwic was also quite awkward, ungifted in the art of small talk. His efforts felt more like intrusions into an employee's personal life than attempts to relate on a human level. He began, "I hear you're not going to make the New Year's party this evening. You know, our office functions are a great way to meet coworkers on a more personal level."

"Not feeling it this year," I said working the screwdriver as quickly as possible but trying to do so without seeming to hurry.

"That's a shame. Well, I'm sure you're looking forward to our generous three-day weekend, at least. And I bet a ladies' man such as you has plenty of activities planned."

I ignored that and kept disconnecting the camera.

He continued. "What do you do when you're not up here at work, hobby-wise, besides entertaining the ladies? Which, of course, you know is your reputation all over the company."

I stopped working and looked at him. "I garden," I said, and went back to dismounting the camera.

"How nice. A green thumb, and what do you grow?"

"Lately? Weeds. I need to get in with a rake and clean it out. But, to be honest, with the way things are going, I haven't felt like keeping up with it."

His voice went silky and he said, "You know that's exactly what we're doing around here. A little seasonal weeding does a business good. Where is your ID badge?"

I said, "I just tucked it into my pocket so it wouldn't get snaggled while I was working."

"Why don't you go ahead and get that back out."

I fixed my ID badge, boxed my tools back up and collected the dismounted camera. "I guess that does it. Have a good day, sir."

"Glad we had a chance to chit-chat," he said. "Always nice."

Everything about him brought me down and brought this company down. But the higher-ups thought he was a rising star. They saw value in him I couldn't find. To me, he destroyed. To them, he created. His watchful eye was just the sort of thing they thought we needed.

I returned to my office and tried to calm myself. Closed my eyes. Meditated for something positive. I asked the Universe to deliver me some solace, some retreat. I needed something wonderful.

My e-mail dinged. It was a note from Mr. Trudgwic. He sent a follow-up that read, "Mr. West, as per our earlier conversation, display your ID badge at all times. Refusal of this compulsory directive is a direct violation of this company's Safety and Security standards. Please reference your employee handbook under the Safety and Security section page 1 if you have any questions or need to schedule a meeting with me on the heretofore mentioned subject, and I will be glad to assist you. Thank you in advance for your complete cooperation."

A crack in the paint caught my eye. I'd never noticed it. I stared at it wishing I could crawl in, blank of mind, scarcely breathing. The second hand clicked loudly on the wall clock behind me. The walls were crushing; the air suddenly too dusty for a fresh breath.

Jose, my coworker from another branch, stuck his head into my office. "Hey, West, wake up! Your order's here. Still missing the cameras though. They're on backorder, but come get your other crap. You're making the New Year's party tonight, right?"

"Give me a break," I said.

"I know what you mean. The Trudge' is a blue-ribbon prick alright, that's for sure. No one in our division can believe how you put up with him. How do you stay so cool?"

"I need my job."

"Don't we all. So you're not making the party?"

"I doubt it. I don't know."

"The girls in HR are going to be disappointed! You can't miss. They all have their eye on you, you know. It won't be the same if you're not there. Say, man, you are really down. You're a wreck. I've never seen you like this. The party might do you good, reconsider, eh? At any rate, everyone's hoping your boy Trudg' don't show, but rumor has it he will. Well, chief, sign for this crap. I've got to get moving."

I sat for a long time after he left considering my options. I turned to the computer and found a website that considers a person's interests and qualifications. I carefully answered all its questions, searching my innermost desires, hoping I'd discover a great job with adequate money and get myself out of here. But when I hit send, wouldn't you know it, this same job came back. I was trapped for certain. I had nine more years to retirement and no telling how much of that would be under Mr. Trudgwic… if I still even had a job after all the disciplinary forms.

A few tickets came in for service, then a few more. But I couldn't bring myself to address them. They sat. I sat feeling as if I awaited the inevitability of my next write-up.

The day dragged on. My pile of tickets sat untouched and the security cameras still had not arrived. One minute after quitting time an e-mail appeared in my inbox. It was from Mr. Trudgwic: "As per our conversation this morning, you once again failed to comply with the company policy of informing the supervisor when vendor orders do not arrive on time. It is imperative…"

I began to fear the worst. This guy was going to wreck my job and make it so I couldn't even transfer branches or even have a reference. I looked over at the pile of tickets and was seized with frantic inspiration. I began to complete each job one-by-one, even taping down wires and air-can dusting computer boxes. I did it up right, top notch, the best I could.

The parking lot began to empty. A few tickets later, I looked again, and I was in the building alone. Within the following hour, all my tickets were done. The only thing that remained was for me to deliver the hard-copy notification to Mr. Trudgwic's office.

My lone foot falls echoed sharply through the empty halls as I approached and opened the cold double doors to the office area. The phones were ringing unanswered, lines blinking out of time. The fish tank lid still rested at the bottom of the tank with several dead fish. I turned towards Mr. Trudgwic's office. His light was on. The door was open. I suddenly became very nervous. I had really hoped he would not be here.

Cautiously I stepped into his office. He was seated at his desk and startled when he saw me. Apparently he thought he was alone as well. He fumbled for his mouse, minimizing a window; behind it was his personal e-mail account, open. I approached his desk, thinking I would drop my paper and leave. He looked extremely agitated and became very clumsy, knocking his mouse to the ground. Was he trying to hide something?

I said to him, "I'll call over to check after the three-day holiday, but the security cameras still aren't here. I have the written notification. Are you okay, sir?"

He jolted forward, bucking hard and loud against his desk like he was stuck hard from the inside. His face strained. His bug eyes bulged even more than usual. His brow twitched and beaded with sweat. He grasped his arm. He seemed torn by needing help and glancing frightfully at his computer monitor, but did not answer. It appeared that he could not speak.

I glanced up at the wires where the security camera had been. They hung out of the wall pitiful, useless, limp. I looked back at him. "You having a heart attack there, Trudgwic?" I already knew the answer.

He nodded his head. My first instinct was to rush over and help him. Call 911. Save his life. But he was so damn ugly, writhing there like a salted slug. The toad who had made such a game of my life twitched in his fancy leather chair which squeaked a sharp farting sound, with his soft underbelly exposed pleading with his eyes for help. Maybe it was the awkwardness of the situation, like when I was young and would see another kid get a spanking or fall down, I burst into laughter. I tried to hold it back, but it made me snot a bit, which really hit me funny.

Holding my side, tearing up and hardly able to speak, I asked, "Would you like me to call an ambulance, Trudg'?"

He gasped and twitched, but did not answer. I got myself under control, wiped my face and eyed him like one eyes the mosquito before smashing it into a bloody paste. "No?" I asked him between fading hiccups of laughter. "Suit yourself."

I took a deep refreshing breath like one does at meditation, and I began to relax for the first time in weeks. I touched my toes and stretched my chest feeling really loose all the sudden. Things felt shockingly right, as if Nature taking her course washed the weight of the world off of me and everything shifted back into alignment. Remembering why I came to his office in the first place, with a wave of my hand I said, "Completely different subject, but here is the paperwork you required. I hope this satisfies the policy."

His eyes widened.

"The camera should be in after the weekend," I continued. "I'll be sure to check first thing with the vendor, after our generous three-day break, of course."

He began to understand the power of karma, I think. Maybe it was his own spiritual awakening. "He...hel...help...mm..." A silver line of saliva stretched from his mouth to his shoulder, my silver lining to the thundercloud of him.

"Yeah, probably a policy against that. Is first aid a part of tech training? I don't think it is. You ever get into meditation and the metaphysical? Since you came aboard here, I have. And they say the Lord never gives you something you can't handle."

"My heart!" It was barely audible, more of a mouthing in a hiss of air.

"Exactly. It's a matter of heart. And they quote that whole jazz about what don't kill you only makes you stronger. Anyway, you got this Ole' T. Brace up! This little heart thing is nothing for a blue-ribbon prick like you. And, incidentally, everyone knows you're a sorry little prick. But just now, there's no one watching you. You, who never looked out for anyone, have no one looking out for you. There's no one here to see. No camera present. A few minutes ago, while you were doing whatever it was you were doing at your desk there, you thought that was a good thing, no doubt. You made me feel like a horse's ass, but now it's you. Consider this a weeding of the company garden, and you're just sideways in the rake."

He shook his head a little, as if astonished by the way he was perceived. As if he had no idea how I felt about him, and I think he was afraid. Yes, he was definitely afraid. And I really couldn't have cared less. I said, "So, can I get a signature indicating that you've received this? No? What were you looking at on your computer screen? I'll wager it wasn't company business. Is that your ID badge on the floor?"

There was no way I'd go behind his desk to see. I'd leave some smudge of evidence, some fact that I'd been here, and truth be told, I really didn't care what he was up to.

But he did. He groaned in horror and slumped back in his chair. Helpless and wrecked.

He horsed out the words: "I hurt... I hurt."

Far off in the background, I could hear the faint sound of the fish tank gurgling out its long silver line of bubbles, and I left him there. They say he died of "natural causes." No one ever mentioned what was on his screen, and of course I could never ask. Maybe it truly was coincidence, but to me, it seemed that when a person begs God or the Universe or whatever you want to call it, hard enough for something, like I did, it delivers.

Funny thing was I almost signed out when I passed through the front office, but shrugged. If T is still here after the break, well, he can write me up then.

I decided to head on over to the company party. After all that excitement, I felt like a six pack and putting on my dancing shoes. Anyway, I'll disappoint the girls from HR if I don't at least make an appearance, and how could I do an awful thing like that?

The Writer

Let's say, I have a "friend" with a sketchy personal life, and he told me that for "those" types (the sketchy types, not like me or my readers), their jobs are their true anchors to upright society. Excellence at work is the one element of life that lets them know they're okay and not complete screw-ups. So, they take their jobs seriously. They work hard and are model employees.

But, when this gets threatened, their whole world quakes.

Once, the two most pathetic human beings on Earth became my boss. (That's boss, singular, because neither could act alone. They were two impotent heads on the same flaccid hydra.) In retrospect, I'm glad it happened because had it not, I'd never have believed such a miserable thing could befall such a wonderful person (me) with so little provocation. I, now, have much more compassion and understanding for those in the same situation.

At the time though, aside from feeling constantly afraid, enraged, stressed, confounded, belittled, embarrassed, nervous, and helpless, it also felt pretty bad.

The only option I had, besides barely surviving the ordeal, was to find satisfaction exacting my revenge through literature. And after I'd written this story, every time the boss pulled me into the office for discipline, to tell me the same ol' jargon, the same ol' rote lines of policy, I had the secret pleasure of my story. I had a simple fantasy, a private construction in my head to play out behind my eyes, a sweetness to temper what was so bitter. So, like my good friend Dennis Flynn used to say, "If you can't kill 'em, Poe 'em."

What I would never do in life, I could do in literature. Besides, it's not illegal (at least not yet), and in my version, I get to come out on top!

The Craft

The opening pages of a novel, or paragraphs of a short story, should introduce the major themes that will be addressed throughout the entire work. Here, I used the image of the dead horse. The character provides the connection by relating the image to his life. I did this with the idea that when we're depressed, we view the world with the lens of depression, and it colors everything. Keep this in mind for your characters. Their feelings should color how they see the world around them.

Remember setting has three parts: time, place, and state-of-mind. Where we are and in what time we are there have power over how we see the world at that moment.

Christopher Vogler mapped this out in his book *The Writer's Journey*, Our characters experience both an inner and an outer journey. The internal journey is an emotional journey that logically complements the exterior events that change the archetypal character from initiate to hero.

Another symbol I used at the beginning was the fish tank. It stands for the workplace. Yet, it is also a place where more aggressive fish—and neglect—kill others in the tank. It is where the "silver lining" that the character will experience at the end is introduced.

When describing the way your character looks, avoid the police description; instead, offer descriptions that in some way reveal their character. It would add little to the story if I described Mr. Trudgwic as 5'10, 173 pounds, a small scar on his elbow, unless I elaborate on how he got the scar. But mentioning his weight and height are stale.

Instead, describe only the details that help reveal character. For example, I gave Trudgwic bug eyes because it infers he sees everything. I paralleled his eyes and the security camera. In contrast, the security camera, upgraded from black-and-white to color, would record the surveillance more clearly and without emotion, while Mr. Trudgwic sees the world in ways that feed his own sadistic pleasures and further his career.

I made the character's boss male because it's less sympathetic for our protagonist to let a woman die, and I wanted (obviously) to keep my character sympathetic. I also had Mr. Trudgwic hiding something on his computer screen, but I never named it exactly. As writers we can leave some things undefined. This gives readers a chance to infer, and it actually creates more tension.

Stephen King said, "Nothing is so frightening as what's behind the closed door...." Recalling that, I wanted to let the computer stand as the "closed door." Though my goal was not to frighten readers, I wanted it to serve as an opportunity for them to make inferences as to what he may have been looking at. This creates tension and demonstrates Trudgwic's possible engagement in illegal activities or, even worse, something against company policy!

The Invitation

Take revenge through literature. If you're obsessing over the way someone has treated you, or you have something so stressful that you harp incessantly about it to your social group, create a plot and confront the situation in fiction. It's safe, and no one gets hurt for real. Also, just as with manipulating a nightmare, this might pull the concept into the tangible world and help you relieve the misery.

But as you do, make sure you keep the sympathy with your character. And since the topic is here, I'll mention that there are several no-no's that story heroes do not do.

A hero may rob, murder, cheat, lie and even torture other characters, and an audience will stay with them. But heroes may not rape, molest a child, or engage in incest. That said, I know once you give an artist a rule, they'll show you how to break it.

Consider how Gorge R. R. Martin, in his *Game of Thrones* series, works with the incest taboo. Characters Cersei and Jamie Lannister (just one of his several incest examples), are sister and brother and secret lovers. Yet, as Hercules was allowed to atone for murdering his wife and children, these characters endure such trials that challenge the reader's own humanity, and we rejoice when they have their victories. But they are generally not our true heroes.

Even the great Oedipus could not remain anything but tragic.

A BETTER PLACE

Keegan sat at his fine oak desk, staring through the large bay window, bouncing his dreams off the brick wall of the warehouse just beyond the narrow alley of his backyard. A thin plastic sack flittered like a gull's wing, trapped half outside of the dumpster lid. But in Keegan's mind, he was at the beach. Large waves pulled surfers across their tops. Children, smiling with eyes half-obscured beneath wind-tossed hair, built drip castles and sand castles and held up broken bits of sand dollars as if they were pirate treasure, and when their parents cautioned them that they had swam too far out, or were being unsafe, they ran back with happy faces and played where their parents asked them to. Keegan loved this beach. It was the first time he had ever been there. It was the first time he had imagined it.

The door to his study creaked open.

"Keegan, dear, your daughter is on her way."

The bricks rebuilt themselves over his beachscape, as he came to. He leaned back in his chair a bit. "Is she bringing her monstrous children?"

"Unfortunately, yes. But don't you get ugly, hear? You pretend they are the darlings she imagines them to be."

"I guess. If people aren't left their fantasies, then what is life's point?"

His wife smiled at him. "You better get loose now. They will be here shortly."

Keegan's non-writing hand was strapped to a handle from which he freed himself, and his feet were in stirrups beneath his desk as if he had been braced to avoid being sucked away by an immense vacuum. He opened his desk drawer and took out a tissue. He wiped a spot of blood that had run between his finger tip and a page in the thick, leather-bound book that rested beneath it. The top third of the page described a beautiful day at a beach. No conflict was yet established, just a lovely description of well-behaved children enjoying themselves near the surf.

A straight razor lay in a kidney-shaped, silver dish at his left. Its blade was made of beautiful Damascus steel; its handle was a polished quartz crystal. A spot of Keegan's blood stood out next to it, in the dish. He wiped this up as well and discarded the tissue into a small trashcan near his desk.

He stood and walked down the stairs to the living room. His wife was reading from a small book at a sitting table near the window. She said, "Remember when you wrote that story about the two trees that lived beneath the kudzu canopy, and they fell in love?"

"And then the kudzu crushed them, and they died," he said. "No, I don't remember that one."

"Oh, yes you do! It chokes me up every time; I love reading it. Those two gnarly old trees are you and me."

"We are always the great lovers. The kudzu is your daughter, and the bed bugs are who she calls her children."

"My daughter?" Natalie said. "Oh no, that's your daughter! Give her credit; at least she is finally on her own."

"Credit?" Keegan snorted. "She has no credit. And she ruined both of ours. We don't have any credit either, by the way."

"There's her car. I hear it turning down the street."

"You can hear that exhaust leak three blocks away. How long do you think it will take her to ransack the kitchen again?"

"You're so negative," Natalie said. "She won't do that. She's grown up now. Besides, what's the big deal?"

"It's how she goes about it. She's just rude, that's all. Bothers me."

A dusty, dented Lincoln hit the curb outside and crunched to a stop. Streams of smoke hissed out from beneath the hood. Three car doors popped open. A woman, thirty-something, carrying a huge purse began clomping up the walk. Her oldest child, a hefty, dirty-faced girl of fifteen went over and helped a crying baby out of its car seat. The other son, a boy of seven, charged up the walk next to his mom, skipping and kicking the tops off the daffodils near the walkway as he passed.

Natalie pulled the curtains aside and watched as they approached.

Keegan said, "I guess I may as well let them in. No avoiding it," and began to rise from his chair. Natalie, seeing the daffodils exploding along their front walk, stopped him. "I'll get the door. You rest there."

"I'll get it. It's okay," Keegan said.

"I'm right here," she said watching flower after flower explode in a fluttering shower of yellow petals. "You rest. I'll get it."

"Nonsense, I'll answer the door."

"Keegan, sit down! I'll get it."

He smiled and sat back down. "You pamper me," he said.

She eyed their daughter though the curtains. "I have to," she said worried.

The bell rang, and Natalie opened the door. "Sandra, come in. Children, come inside. Sit over there. I'll have some iced tea ready in a moment."

Sandra dropped her purse hard onto the floor and plopped down onto the sofa. "Sweet tea, I hope, with those lemon wheels you used to do. I love that. Do you have anything to eat around here? Kids, get in the kitchen and make a few sandwiches. Do up some for the road too, and bring them to Momma. I'll pack them here in my purse. What a day! I tell you, I need a vacation. I need to get away for a while. And come here you two, give us a kiss!"

Natalie looked at her with what appeared to be great interest as Sandra spoke. "A vacation, wouldn't that be nice? Poor thing is stressed to high heaven. Where would you like to go, dear?"

"The beach," she said, "or anywhere, I don't care, just anywhere for a while. Do you have any toilet paper? I'm out. I think little Bennie starts wiping at his ankle before he hits the business, if you know what I mean. The little guy will burn through a roll in three days."

Keegan smiled and blinked, "That is fascinating, darling. What are your plans for today? You must be very busy. You can probably only stay for a short while."

"Oh, I don't have be anywhere," Sandra said and leaned back.

"Nowhere to be?" Keegan asked.

"Nowhere at all," she said, relaxing.

At that moment little Bennie leapt over the back side of the couch. He leaned in to Natalie and screamed like an elephant right into her ear, jolting her with surprise.

"I'm an elephant! I'm an elephant! I'm a hippopotamus!" he shouted throwing his arms over his head, then roared into her ear again. "I'm heavy aren't I, mamaw! And look how high I can jump on your lap!"

Sandra continued speaking as if nothing had happened, "Yep, we have all day to spend with the fam. Just us. All day. Nowhere to be."

Bennie wiped a booger off his finger onto the upholstery and crawled off the sofa. Then he charged off someplace else in the house.

Natalie looked at Keegan, who did the eyebrow thing they used to communicate silently "things" that should not be communicated aloud. In this case, it was Keegan saying, "Come up with a reason to get them out of here, NOW!" Through the years Natalie learned to never ignore this. She immediately said, "Well, I wish we had all day, darling, but we have so many things to do, we'd better keep our visit rather short this afternoon."

Sandra said, "No biggie then. Listen up kids, change of plans! We're kicking this pit stop into high gear. Darla, get on upstairs and stand under that shower head for a few. We don't have all day for visiting."

Bennie ran over to Keegan, "What happened to your finger? Did you cut it? It's ugly! Your fingers are always cut up, and it's gross."

Keegan leaned in so Natalie couldn't hear him and said, "How about I stick this gnarly finger in your pink little ear?"

Bennie screamed and ran away.

Natalie crinkled her nose and said, "Sandra, I think your baby needs changing."

"Did she bust a duce, again? She's been squirting like a sick goose all morning. Must have been that funnel cake I gave her for breakfast. You know they put up such fun little carnivals there in the parking lot there off... It's at that mall over there by... Well, it's I-10 and something."

"Should you give an infant leftover funnel cake for breakfast?" Natalie asked.

"Apparently not!" Keegan replied, as if she had actually asked him instead of Sandra.

Bennie shouted from the top of the stairs, "What's this knife Grandpa? It looks sharp! It was on this book. I can't read good yet, but there's writing in it. I can see it!" He held up the book in his other hand. "This book smells salty. It smells gross." He dropped the book, and it fell open to the page Keegan had been working on. Bennie looked down at it, then back at the razor. He hinged the long blade out slowly. "So sharp! So very sharp!"

Keegan hopped up. "Put that down, Bennie."

"No! Bennie! Put that knife down," Natalie said.

"Where's Bennie?" Sandra said.

"Put the knife down, sweetheart. Listen to your grandfather," Natalie said.

"Drop that razor, and get down here," Keegan shouted.

"Hey, don't yell at my baby! Who said you could shout at him like that?" Sandra said finally looking up to see what all the commotion was about. "Oh my, God! Bennie, you little idiot! Drop that razor, now! Mommy said now! I'm going to beat your butt into next week!"

Keegan started forward. "Now, Bennie, you put that down. That is not a toy."

Sandra stopped him. "Keegan, please, I'll handle this. He's my son."

"But, you don't understand," Keegan started.

"Please, I'm the mother here, and I understand perfectly. Please. He's my son. I'm the disciplinarian."

"He's going to…"

"I'm the disciplinarian! Not you, thank you very much!" She pushed past Keegan and raced towards the stairs. "You put that down, Bennie!"

"So very sharp!" Bennie said. "I'll just touch the blade a little bit, just a little bit, but only on the edge, so sharp, just the…"

Keegan and Natalie glanced at one another, temporarily frozen with disbelief. Natalie said, rather weakly, "Listen to your mother, Bennie."

"I've cut myself!" Bennie shouted. "Oh, it burns!" He started to cry. "I've cut myself real bad!" He sat down. His bloody hand rested on the page of the open book, and he lay down.

Keegan said, "Sandra, look what you've done! You let him hurt himself. You have to watch after him!"

Sandra stopped moving towards her injured son and turned around. "I will not be insulted by you, Keegan, when he's the one that went and got that razor. He cut himself! How am I to blame? A razor which you left out, I might add! I say it's your fault he cut himself."

Natalie said, "Sandra, it's rude to address your father by his name. Don't do that, dear."

"We never would have done that in my day," Keegan said. "You kids have no respect anymore, but boy howdy do you expect to receive it!"

"Well," Sandra said, crossing her arms, "I'm just not about to take blame for something I didn't do is all. What I think rude is to go about casting blame... Keegan!"

Staring up towards the top of the stairs, Natalie said, "Oh my, Bennie has disappeared."

"He's what?" asked Keegan.

"He has disappeared."

"Bennie?" Sandra asked. "Oh, Bennie! Mommy's coming, baby!"

"Disappeared?" Keegan asked. "You mean as in, he's with the kudzu?"

"Yes, the kudzu," Natalie replied.

"Oh, my" Keegan said. "Then he has disappeared."

Sandra raced back up to where Bennie had been. "Disappeared, my Bennie? Oh, *no*! Bennie, baby, now is not the time for hide-and-seek. Bennie? Ben-eeeee!"

At the top of the stairs Sandra saw Keegan's book and open razor, but no sign of her sweet, little Bennie. Downstairs Keegan and Natalie could hear her rumbling around looking in the bedroom, the study, the closet. She flung open the bathroom door.

"Darla, where is Bennie? Is he hiding in here? What are you doing? What the heck are you doing to yourself?"

Darla raised such a riot of cursing along with shouting, "Get out! Get out of here!" that it was obvious he had not gone in there. Sandra came back down the stairs, plopped onto the sofa and began to sob.

"I can't find my Bennie anywhere, and he's hurt!" She jumped up again and shouted, "Bennie! Come down to Mommy. You're not being funny!"

Natalie put her hand on Sandra's leg. "It's okay, dear."

Keegan agreed. "It's not as bad as you might think. He's fine."

"What do you mean? He's hurt himself and now he's gone. He's gone! He can't be fine."

"No." said Natalie. "He's fine. He's… in a better place. He's happy now."

"He's not dead!" Sandra shouted. "He's gone!"

"No, not dead," Keegan said.

"Where's my other baby?" Sandra asked and picked up her infant. She sat it between her legs, holding it. The power of the dirty diaper hit her all at once. "Whew, lordy!"

"We don't keep extra diapers," Natalie said. "We don't wear them yet."

"Use a dish towel," Keegan said, "and some duct tape if you have to." Of course he was joking.

"Oh, shabby chic. I like that idea," Sandra said.

"So about Bennie," Natalie started. "He's cut himself with no ordinary razor."

"Cripes!" Sandra shouted, wiping up the baby, paying very little attention to her mother. "No more funnel cake for you. Gag me with a turd… literally. My goodness!"

"It's a magic razor," Keegan said. "Sandra, are you listening?"

"Tell her where you got it, dear," Natalie said.

"You kids never listen anymore," Keegan said.

"Sandra, listen to your father about his magic razor."

274

"Is she even listening?"

"Oh, God, it's on my hand!" Sandra said.

"Listen to your father, dear. Go on, honey."

"I've got to wash my hand."

Keegan continued, "I've owned it for a long time, since my travels through the Middle East. I bought it from a man who had, at the very moment I met him, sworn an oath to never cut his beard again. He gave it to me for a fair price."

"Right, for religious reasons," Natalie said, "and a very fair price."

Sandra looked at them. "That's really, fascinating... really. A magic razor... Would you like to see the magic carpet I flew over on? It's just out front here."

Darla came out of the bathroom with one towel around her body and another on her head. "Grandma, you need bigger towels! I can hardly stretch this over my stomach."

Sandra shouted up, "You mean your chest don't you, honey?"

"No, Mom. I don't have a chest. It's my stomach! Instead of boobs I got a big, fat gut. Did anyone ever make sandwiches or tea?"

Keegan said, "You better wait up there. Don't come down here yet. We need to get that razor and book up."

"But I'm thirsty, Grandpa," she said and kept walking. "And I'm hungr... ouch! I just cut my foot. My towel fell off! It's deep! Who left a razor... Bennie! You little idiot. Did you leave a razor in middle of the floor. Mom! Oh, my, I have to sit down. Where's my towel..."

"Darla!" Sandra shouted. "Darla, honey! Are you okay?"

"Mom, I cut my foot on a razor Bennie left out! I'm not bleeding on the carpet though. I have it over this book here to catch the blood."

"No! Honey," Natalie said. "You'd better stay away from any kind of paper, but, you go on and bleed on the carpet. It's okay."

"Well, if you can, maybe, catch a little bit on the book." Keegan said.

"You be quiet," Natalie said.

"I cut myself! I can't be quiet," Darla said.

"Not you Darla, Keegan. Darla, you bleed on the carpet. It's all right, darling."

"I'll bleed on this book," Darla said.

Keegan said, "You better listen to your grandma, Darla."

Sandra shouted, "Darla, how bad is it? I'm coming, honey! Mommy is on her way!"

Sandra ran back up to the top of the stairs. "Darla! Darla? Dar-laaaaaaaa! Where are you baby?"

Natalie and Keegan looked at one another.

"With the kudzu?" Natalie asked.

"With the kudzu," Keegan said.

"What the heck is going on around here? What is kudzu? Where are my babies? Where's my son, my daughter?"

Natalie stood and walked up stairs. She pushed the two wet towels crumpled on the ground aside and picked up the book and Keegan's razor. She brought them downstairs. Keegan held out his hand to receive them, but Sandra snatched them away.

"Now see here!" Keegan said.

Natalie said, "Dear, you'd better give those back to your father."

Sandra opened the book and read over the most recent entry. "What's this story here about a beach trip with two kids, one naked, running wild in the surf with no adult supervision? You are writing ugly stories about my babies!"

"Of course not, dear," Natalie said.

"No, definitely not," Keegan said.

"Oh, yeah, then why are their names Bennie and Darla? And what's the deal with this razor?" She sat the book down next to her baby, who was sitting on the floor upright, bobbling around, not yet altogether strong enough to sit upright for long. Sandra opened the razor.

"Don't do that, darling," Keegan said.

"Listen to your father now," Natalie said.

"Interesting blade," Sandra said. "What are all those waves in the metal?"

"That's the steel," Keegan said. "They fold it."

"It's from Damascus," Natalie added.

"Looks sharp," Sandra said.

"It's very sharp. Give it back to your father, dear," Natalie said.

"Sandra, put it down, or give it to me," Keegan said. "It will pull you through. You're not strapped down. Listen to me. For once in your life, listen!"

"Aren't you bossy today!" Sandra said. "I'm a grown woman, and I can feel this thing all over if I want, tip to top! But I'm not. I'm only going to touch the blade a little bit. Just the edge. Ouch!"

Surprised, she dropped the open razor. It tumbled down, flashing in the light, and nicked the baby's leg before settling on the carpet. The baby immediately started crying.

"I actually just cut myself. It burns! And I've cut my baby! I'm a terrible parent!" Sandra reached down with her cut hand and grabbed the baby's tiny, nicked leg in an effort to stop the bleeding, which really was an overreaction. The baby's cut was not very bad.

Keegan was completely irritated by this. "If you don't listen... Why can't you ever listen?"

"I've cut my baby! I can't believe I just did that."

"You really should have listened," Natalie said.

"Listening has nothing to do with it!" Sandra said. "I've just cut myself and my baby. Can you not hear me?"

Sandra grabbed the baby's leg and felt the bite of her cut. She winced a little which knocked the baby over; its fat little leg fell across the page which opened up into the great yawning vacuum of a never-ending hole. Instantly sucked in, the baby disappeared. Sandra screamed and tried to reach into the page and pull the baby free. Her grab was so frantic and overextended that she upset herself from the couch and was powerfully inhaled into the hole as well. Keegan's book flipped a few pages with the vacuum then shut.

Keegan and Natalie sat in their suddenly very quiet living room.

"Are they at the beach?" she asked at length.

Keegan picked up the book and skimmed a few pages. "Yes. They are at the beach."

"That's nice," Natalie said. "Didn't Sandra say she wanted to go to the beach?"

Keegan nodded. "It looked like a nice place."

"Well," Natalie said, "maybe we can check up on them sometime."

Keegan said. "I'll burn the pages in a few weeks, and they'll come back. We'll give her a nice break for a while."

"Anything you want to add to their story, while they are there?" Natalie asked.

Keegan smiled and touched his cut finger. "I'll write a lesson into it that she'll never forget."

"But, Keegan, dear, don't you do anything too dark."

"It's me! You know I wouldn't."

"Exactly, and I know you would! How about some sandwiches and iced tea? I'm feeling a little piqued." Natalie rose and headed towards the kitchen. "How was your story from this morning going to end?"

"I was going to have you and me rich and free from the rude, demanding world and all its troubles, with only one another to love and be concerned for, in a better place."

"We always were the great lovers," Natalie said. "I like that story."

She began to prepare a couple of sandwiches and glasses of her lemon wheel iced tea for just the two of them.

The Writer

When I was a kid, my dad trained me to not speak if he said to be quiet for fear someone might be in the house. It was important.

One day, I took a trip to both Walmart and IKEA in the same day, the same hellish day. The kids in IKEA tore up the bed displays, wrestling. At Walmart, they screamed, standing in their carts like twelve-pound sea captains cursing in the face of a hurricane. The chaos these families live with had worked itself like a wart—a virus that tricks the host body into thinking it's a part of it—warping what these dazed parents considered normal.

Everyone around hated the behavior, but they all turned away with absently sour looks, helpless to do anything but endure it. Because if anyone had spoken up, those parents would have finally had the scapegoats they needed to vent their miseries on.

With this in mind, I created the daughter's character.

The Craft

I began with a simply stated premise: kids don't listen to their parents anymore.

It's a generalized premise, but for my purposes it was accurate enough. As James Joyce said, short stories move towards a single epiphany, so I didn't want to convolute it by contrasting good parenting styles with bad ones. I wanted it simple, like a fable or a parable. It's an example. And I wanted to make it humorous. Because objectively, it's hilarious that an adult, who would leap into battle with anyone who dared to correct them, could be so absolutely controlled by someone 100% dependent on them.

Keegan's mysterious straight razor introduces a touch of magical realism. I used two clichés:

- artists who talk of "pouring themselves" onto the page, or into their art.
- writers who say, "It's as if the story just wrote itself!"

I literally interpreted these and gave these qualities to Keegan.

I also use unsympathetic characters. Sandra and her family have few redeeming qualities, but they're not so bad that we hate them. They're just obnoxious. So, when they all disappear from their completely chaotic lives, and go on a magical beach vacation, we are glad for them. I also set a timeframe so they can come back.

Consider this:

You can conduct psychological experiments in literature. Consider, for example, Sir William Golding's *Lord of the Flies*. He took a load of English school boys and crash-landed them on a pristine island. Society's thin agreement was soon replaced with contrasting philosophies of survival. The choir boys (stereotypically the most moral and well behaved of children) became the worst. But at the end, when they all see the officer walking up the beach—the symbol of the empire—they stop and are ashamed. It's a timeless experiment into human depravity.

Sir Arthur Conan Doyle received death threats when he killed off Sherlock Holmes, and though he grew tired of writing him, he brought Holmes back! Stephen King in *Misery* created an author who, in fiction, faced a situation similar to Doyle's real one, but King imagined his character captured by an obsessed fan and tortured into writing a work with the ending she wanted. King again conducted another experiment in his short story "Survivor Type" in which his premise asked how far a person would go to survive—even self-cannibalizing. In my favorite line of the story he says, "You are what you eat, and I haven't changed a bit!"

These explorations into humanity make excellent literature. But, they begin with a premise and a lesson. They don't just tell a story; they explore an idea.

The Invitation

Write a story that clearly stays on premise. What aspect of humanity would you like to explore? Is there a lesson you want to share, or a point you want to make? As you write have all of your mechanisms tasked with pushing your story toward that theme. Stay on message.

Use repetition. Have characters echo one another, and let their dialogue reflect an interaction. Listen to how the people around you pick up sayings from one another and repeat what they hear on the news (sometime verbatim); have your story people do the same.

Also if you find that your stories run too short, you may not have relaxed into the "showing" of them. Your writing may seem aloof and distant. Write, instead, describing with imagery (using all the senses often, but not all at the time). Scour your stories for "telling" moments, and revise them into moments of detail that connect back into the characters, and back into the theme.

APPENDIX A

A SAMPLE ANALYSIS OF A CLASSIC MYTH

A brief analysis of classic myth will reveal the multilayered lessons that they present. These too, can be considered when writing our own pieces.

For example, take the commonly known myth of Persephone, goddess of maidenhood and vegetation.

The surface of the myth:

One of the ultimate virgins of mythology, she is a young and fresh girl out picking flowers in a field. Her mother Demeter, goddess of the harvest, who provided the grains and fertility of the earth, was not far away.

Hades, on his black chariot, crashes up through the earth and steals Persephone, dragging her like a seed, back down into the earth.

Demeter, in her sorrow, refuses to create seeds or fertilize those made, and lets the world begin to die.

Meanwhile, Hades fails to persuade Persephone to love him, as she misses the flowers of earth and her mother. He plies her with jewels and metals, the closest things to flowers he can offer from deep within the earth. But she is not happy.

Ultimately, after denying feast after feast, hunger overcomes her, but still, she allows herself to eat only six pomegranate seeds.

In the end, before the world can completely die, the gods intervene, and strike a deal with Hades. Since she ate six seeds, she must return to the underworld for half the year. And she may return to the earth for the other half of the year. And this is where we get our seasons.

Other messages within the myth:

Looking more closely, we find a warning from the ancient Greeks arguing that it is unnatural for a married woman never to see her family. Nor is it natural for her to live with her family all the time once married. Without a healthy balance, the protagonist's world will begin to die, or she will never mature to have a family of her own.

Perhaps that balance is a bit of a barter between the husband (the new family) and her birth family.

Also it is a story about growing up, moving from childhood to adulthood, from the point-of-view of Persephone. The world will not allow her to remain a child forever, and one day she will leave home. However, what truly pleases her remains static. Her status as Queen of the Underworld was no substitute for simply lounging outside, enjoying the natural perfumes and colors of the fertile, blooming field.

To a lesser point we, like Persephone, retreat inside during winter, emerging more comfortably during the warmer months. As the temperature drops outside, it rises at home (so to speak), with most babies being born in the summer, as well as most marriages… though preferably not in that order.

The seed motif works tightly through the myth, as well. Persephone is a virgin, the symbol of maidenhood, untilled, and fertile; so of course, after her marriage to (or rape by) Hades, she is also goddess of vegetation, now a mother herself, forever young, perpetuating generations.

So how do we, as writers, work that many layers and angles into our own myths? I have no idea. I have no idea how to do it with the conscious mind, at least. Perhaps it's the subconscious that adds layers and levels instinctively, and it's the astute reader who teases them out for examination. These are, after all, multi-textual, multi-generational works by many authors.

The characters of the gods are prototypical examples of humanity interacting in stories that demonstrate universal truth. As we study how to emulate them, we search too for deeper discoveries seeded beyond the surface.

APPENDIX B

EXPERIMENT WITH YOUR ART

Ask what defines your art. Explore what you believe its boundaries are. Writing is most often a solitary activity, so collaborating with others can offer an enjoyable mingling of styles, perspectives and points-of-view. Some of the products you co-create will be surprising and cool, as they may be so far out of your normal range.

To offer a few ideas for your own projects, I'll share with you some of mine:

- I co-wrote my first two novels. We took the long way around, and did a lot of things wrong, but we explored our own processes, taught one another a lot about writing, and we had a great time meeting and outlining the works. Without that writing partner, I would have never had the courage to take on my own novel.

THE INVITATION
Try co-writing with a friend. Keep notes, decide who'll do the first draft, and who will do the revisions. Then reconvene to evaluate the next draft together, making any adjustments, debating how things should be done. When you publish, list your names alphabetically to avoid any awkwardness. Who's first and who's last doesn't matter in the long run. You'll each rise or fall on your individual accomplishments apart from the collaboration.

- Multi-genre collaborations are also exciting. I worked with Ryan Harris, a singer/songwriter friend of mine, in a project we recorded called *Two Line: A Beggar's Dozen*, enjoying the edges of what makes a song a song, or a poem a poem. We each agreed that there was a difference, but found it rather difficult to pin down. He also saw aspects to a few of my poems that I hadn't noticed or appreciated the way he did. He considered them as lyrics, making some pretty cool songs out of them. The pieces he and I created (and reinterpreted) together, are still some of my favorites, to this day.

- I recorded some pieces with an experimental musician friend of mine, Keith Krause. He has an amazing finger-style blues. He also uses electronic drums, has a pickup that can sound like a thousand different instruments on his guitar, and rips some of the strangest scales you ever heard. Live, he played a dobro behind me while I read. It was a blast. We called our project *Chris Wise and the Bottom Dwellers* (plural, dwellers; I introduced him as "a man so filthy, he had to be plural!" though he was the only one there). It was incredibly fun!

- My youngest brother, who has his PhD in conducting, took three of my poems ("I Walk," "Gravity," and "The Pilgrim Within") and wrote a portion of his senior recital around them. He was the first senior in three years to write original work for a recital. He had a choir, himself on a grand piano, and a percussionist, with me doing the reading, in front of a few hundred people. It was high stakes and amazing--especially since I don't read music. If this didn't go over well, he wouldn't graduate—a fact he might have considered before asking me. Naturally, he started to worry and asked, "If you can't read music, how do you know where in the score you need to be when you need to be there?" I told him what I heard a drummer for Elton John tell this guy I played a show with at Club Da Da in Dallas, "It'll groove, baby!"

I created my own notation, and we nailed it. It was killer, and it's all on video.

- I've worked with a variety of female poets, as well. Exploring masculine and feminine voices (with me reading the masculine voice, believe it or not), and how they work together in a single vignette.

THE INVITATION

- Work with poets of different genders and energies. Conceive the best scenarios for your chemistry that makes you both shine. Remember, the first rule of comedy is always make your partner look good! Consider the conflict. What's at tension? How do you portray it, and what's the audience's take-away?

- Work with a musician. Not as someone merely backing you up, but as someone co-creating a live experience with you. Bleed around and through one another. And while you're on stage, look like you're having a great time! It's contagious. The crowd will enjoy it, too.

- Try having someone else perform your work. Often times they'll find an angle on it that you didn't see before. And, pretend to be appreciative if they completely massacre it! Not everyone will "do it right" or impress you with your work. But, man it's cool when they do!

APPENDIX C

About the Title

I chose the title for two reasons.

Reason 1: Orion was a giant—the greatest hunter of Greek myth. So, when he threatened to kill every wild beast in the world, the gods took him seriously. They sent Scorpio, a giant scorpion, to kill Orion before he could carry out his threat, and Scorpio was successful. Scorpio, in the night sky, lays directly across the wheel from Orion, like a complementary color that cancelled him out.

I think this myth makes the point to all humanity that no matter our skills, our lofty ambitions, our best intentions, we each have our own scorpion. The size of the scorpion, for the myth, is irrelevant. It was giant because Orion was giant— it is entertaining for the story. Young scorpions actually have as much venom as adults. The ancients would have known that their sting was as potent, so the interpretation of what it means for us must lie elsewhere.

Like Orion with his shield forward and his great bronze club to the rear, the scorpion has its claws forward and its tail curled over its end. It is armored, as is Orion. These details equate them.

The scorpion is a direct response; it is Orion's self-made creature of nightmare, his perfect foil, himself. Scorpio was only dispatched after Orion's boasting. Even at the story's surface, he brought it on himself.

In an earlier piece of the myth, Orion was blind, then he saw. We are all blind to our shortcomings, but once we see them, we can address and strengthen them. This is argued in the same spirit that Oedipus[44] was sighted but metaphorically blind. Then blinded, but metaphorically sighted.

---

[44] Oedipus is the main character in the tragedy *Oedipus Rex* written in 403 B.C. by Sophocles. Oedipus, the King of Thebes, unwittingly killed his father and married his mother. To atone, he stuck out his eyes and went into voluntary exile.

As writers, we all have our scorpions. To survive them, we must discover what makes good writing, examine the techniques in our own works and revise them so that they reflect our ever-changing philosophy of what good writing is.

Reason 2: In 2012, I met my scorpion on a back road in Colorado. As Orion was blind, I am color blind. Basically, some shades of red and green look the same to me. I cannot know if the green potato plants with their broad white flowers blended with the red stop sign and its broad white letters, but I didn't see it. Out in the middle of nowhere, I ran a stop sign. And, everyone was there.

I was double T-boned on the left and right side at 65 mph. The impact on the passenger's side was so great my 10,000 pound truck was thrown high enough that the rear driver's side wheel was embedded in the engine compartment of the truck that smashed the other side. My truck was crushed to the frame from the crew cab back.

The wrecker driver said he'd never seen anything like it and told me that intersection was the most dangerous in the county. I see why.

The miracle of it is that no one was killed. Three trucks, with all that astounding energy, and we all lived.

The next day, after I'd gotten a rental and continued forward on to sunset, I found myself driving right into the belly of Orion. So my scorpion must wait. For now, my journey continues, and I remain to write about it.

GLOSSARY

alliteration is the repetition of initial sounds, usually a consonant, in a group of words next to or near each other, such as Peter Piper, leaping lizards, and Betty's banter did not bother Bobby. Contrast this with consonance and assonance which occur within the words such as the "r" sound in Peter Piper, and the "e" sound in "Peter, Betty's."

anaphora is the repetition of a word or phrase at the beginning of successive verses, clauses or sentences. Examples of this are Dr. Martin Luther King's "I Have a Dream" speech or Julius Caesar's "*Veni, Vidi, Vici*" ("I came; I saw; I conquered.").

assonance is vowel sounds within a word. For example, "Stopping by Woods on a Snowy Evening" by Robert Frost opens with the line "He gives his harness bells a shake."

asyndeton is the purposeful omission of coordinate conjunctions (for, and, nor, but, or, yet, so) for syntactical effect. Contrast to polysyndeton, which is the purposeful addition of conjunctions for syntactical effect.

chiasmus is a Latin term from the Greek meaning "crossing." Chi is the Greek letter X. So a chiasmus a rhetorical term referring to the inversion in the second of two parallel phrases such as in Oscar Hammerstein's line from *Cinderella*, "Do I love you because you're beautiful? Or are you beautiful because I love you?"

cliché is an overworked and unoriginal phrase. Clichéd is its adjective.

consonance is the repetition of consonant sounds produced by consonants within a word, sentence, or phrase. For example, in the poem "Stopping by Woods on a Snowy Evening" by Robert Frost, line twelve reads, "Of easy wind and downy flake."

dialogue tags denote which character is speaking. For example, "Get busy writing that story," Chris said.

diction refers to specific word choice.

didactic refers to writing that is intended to teach.

douzain is a twelve line stanza or poem.

ekphrastic poetry is poetry written about or in response to another work of art.

enjambment is the continuation of a sentence or clause beyond the line break to create audible interest.

euphemism is a mild or pleasant word or phrase that is used instead of one that is unpleasant or offensive.

explicit theme refers to a theme that is clearly stated.

extended metaphor is a metaphor that has been introduced and developed throughout all or part the literary work.

first person singular point-of-view is a narrative told by a character who is speaking about themselves.

foil is a character   with the protagonist.

heterographs are words that have the same pronunciation but different meaning and spelling, such as sun (the star of our solar system) and son (a male child).

heteronyms are words that have the same spelling but have different meaning and pronunciation, such as wind (noun, breeze) and wind (verb, twist). The different pronunciation of words with the same spelling (as in the example) make these different from homonyms.

homonyms are words that have the same spelling and pronunciation but different meanings, such as shore (noun, land along the edge of water) and shore (verb, to prop up). The same pronunciation of different meaning words that are spelled the same (as in the example) make these different from heteronyms.

hyperbole is an exaggerated statement or claim not meant to be taken literally.

idiom is an expression whose meaning cannot be predicted from the words that make it. This can be a saying that is dialectical, regional, or characteristic of a particular era or person.

indirect characterization is character information revealed through his thoughts, words, and actions, or through how other characters respond to, or think about, him.

Irony is using words in a manner that gives them an opposite meaning or an action that has the opposite result from that which was intended. There are three major types of irony:

- Situational
- Verbal
- Dramatic

juxtaposition is setting two unalike things in a scene to contrast one another for artistic statement.

meter, meaning measure in Greek, is a premeasured pattern of stressed and unstressed syllables. These units of collected patterns, when considered individually, are called poetic feet. Pentameter, for example, is a line of five (penta-) metric feet.

English poetry employs five basic meters:

- iambic meter (unstressed/stressed)
- trochaic meter (stressed/unstressed)

- spondaic meter, (stressed/stressed)
- anapestic meter (unstressed/unstressed/stressed)
- dactylic meter (stressed/unstressed/unstressed)

misprision is the misreading or misunderstanding of a text.

motif is a recurrent subject, theme, idea or pattern in literature.

nonce symbols are symbols created by the writer that are unique to the occasion of the poem.

octave is a verse form consisting of eight lines, usually written as two stanzas of abba abba.

onomatopoeia is a word that imitates the sound of a thing like whisper, buzz, splat, drip, splash, howl, and whine.

pastiche is an artistic work that imitates another style, work, or period. But not in a way that makes fun of it. That would be a parody. Pastiche can also be a patchwork, or assembly of pieces to form a literary work.

personification – giving human characteristics to inanimate objects.

polysyndeton – use of conjunctions between every word in a series of words(see asyndeton).

pun is a word play that relies on the different possible meanings of a word.

Q. How many ears does Daniel Boone have?
   A. His left ear, his right ear, and his wild front ear!
   Q. How many ears does Dr. Spock have?
   A. His left ear, his right ear, and his final front ear!

quatrain is a four-line poem or stanza.

rhythm is the pattern of stressed and unstressed syllables in a line of verse. In speech this is natural.

sestet is a unit of verse containing six lines.

setting in literature is used to identify the time, place and mood of a story.

shift in poetry, also called the turn or the volta, indicates a change in the speaker's understanding, tone, or emotion.

situational irony is when actions have the exact opposite effect of what was intended, and the outcome is contrary to what was expected. See irony.

simile is comparison between two different things using "like" or "as."

slam is poetry performance of original material where contestants are judged by pre-selected audience members and rated on a 1-10 scale, decimal points accepted, usually for a cash prize.

slant rhyme is using two words that do not rhyme but have similar sounds. See assonance and consonance.

stanza, meaning "room" in Italian, is a grouped set of lines in a poem usually set off from other stanzas with a line space or an indentation.

syllabic verse – verse lines based on syllables, whether or not they are stressed in a particular pattern.

tercet is a three-line stanza.

triggering subject is a subject that causes the initial writing of the poem.

turn is the point at which a poem moves in a decidedly new direction while maintaining the integrity of the previous writing. See Shift.

volta. See shift.

BIBLIOGRAPHY

Blamires, Steve. *The Irish Celtic Magical Tradition*. London, Thorsons, 1995.

Campbell, Joseph. *The Hero with a Thousand Faces*. Novato, CA, New World Library, 2008.

Dwyer, J.J. "Did Shakespeare Read Dante? A Comparative Inquiry." *The Tablet*, 9 July 1955, p. 9.
Frey, James N. *How to Write a Damn Good Novel*. New York, St. Martin's Press, 1987.

Frey, James N. *How to Write a Damn Good Novel, II: Advanced Techniques for Dramatic Storytelling*. New York, NY, St. Martin's Press, 1994.

Guerber, H. A. *Myths of the Norsemen: From the Eddas and the Sagas*. New York, NY, Dover Publications, 1992.

Hope, Ken. "Introduction on Catullus." *Catullus - Catullus Translations - About Catullus - Gaius Valerius Catullus*, rudy.negenborn.net/catullus/about_cat.htm.

Kurland, Philip B. "Chapter 15, Document 61." *The Founders' Constitution*, vol. 1, University of Chicago, Chicago, 1987.

Levin, Phillis. *The Penguin Book of the Sonnet: 500 Years of a Classic Tradition in English*. London, Penguin, 2002.

Rexroth, Kenneth, translator. *One Hundred Poems from the Chinese*. New York, New Directions Pub., 2013.

Vogler, Christopher. *The Writer's Journey: Mythic Structure for Writers*. 3rd ed., Studio City, Ca, Michael Wiese, 2007.

Yeats, William Butler. *The Collected Poems of W.B. Yeats.* Edited by Richard J. Finneran, New York, Scribner Paperback Poetry, 1996.

Yeats, William Butler. *Selected Poems and Two Plays of William Butler Yeats.* Edited by Macha Louis Rosenthal, New York, Collier Books a Division of Macmillan Publishing Co., 1978.

Zurndorfer, Harriet Thelma. *Chinese Women in the Imperial Past: New Perspectives.* Leiden, Brill, 1999.

Made in the USA
Columbia, SC
27 May 2018